Exploring Southern Oregon's Beautiful Places

by John Kemper

Photographs by the Author

Outdoor Press
Medford, Oregon

ISBN 0-9722509-1-3

DEDICATION:

**To our daughter, Kathy,
and her family, Paul and Heather;
and to my wife, Bobbie
who served as my editor and photographic consultant;**

**and a special thanks to Dr. Frank Lang,
who read the manuscript, and helped me with wildflower identification**

OTHER NATURE BOOKS BY THE SAME AUTHOR:

Southern Oregon's Bird Life
2002, Outdoor Press

Birding Northern California
1999, Globe Pequot Press

Discovering Yolo County Wildlife
1996, Yolo Audubon Society and Yolo Basin Foundation

FRONTISPIECE: Mount McLoughlin

Contents

Contents (continued)

Introduction
What this book is about

Without sounding too much like a Chamber of Commerce representative, I'm going to say right at the outset that southern Oregonians live in an earthly paradise. This doesn't mean that other parts of the northwest could not also be called paradises. Certainly, the entire coastline could qualify, and so could the Columbia Gorge and the high mountains of the Olympics and the Cascades. But Southern Oregon has one of the best parts of the coast, and the Siskiyous and southern Cascades have a combination of accessibility and beauty that makes them special.

This is a book that combines scenery with natural history. Other things of interest, such as cultural events, historical sites, restaurants, hotels, hiking, biking, and rafting, are well covered by other books. Hiking is not excluded; in fact, a number of places in this book involve a modest amount of hiking. Most of the places are reachable by paved roads, although a few may involve gravel roads.

Many people who travel the busy I-5 corridor little realize that some of the best areas in Oregon lay just a short distance away on either side of the highway -- marvelous subalpine slopes, great meadows, and lakes. And one of the best of the best -- the North Umpqua River -- often gets overlooked perhaps because it isn't perceived as a connecting route.

I consider myself to be something of a coastline "junkie," and have sought out beautiful coastlines throughout North America, from Alaska to Maine. I'm prepared to make a statement: the Southern Oregon coastline is the most beautiful of any I have seen. Since I've not seen every coastline in the world, I cannot make a similar statement that it is *the* most beautiful coastline in the world. But I'll bet it is, just the same.

My purpose in this book is to try to call attention to such special places, and to encourage other people to appreciate them. My emphasis, as already stated, is on natural history, because much of the pleasure in being in scenic surroundings is to know more about the plants and animals who live there. This book does not try to cover every possible place of interest, but concentrates on those places that I think qualify as "beautiful places."

There are lots of wildflowers in this book, and even some cultivated flowers. Many of the flowers that today are growing wild, such as sweetbriar roses and sweet peas, were once in somebody's garden. Many are "aliens" from Europe or Asia, growing wild. I have not discriminated against inclusion of "alien" plants, asking only that they be attractive. I have not tried to pin down every wildflower as to exact species. I learned early that there are some close lookalikes in the plant kingdom, which can be identified with precision only by experts. In an appendix, I have shown some of the common names that have been given to wildflowers, plus the scientific names.

My rather artificial definition of "Southern Oregon" includes the coast from Reedsport south to the California Border, and as far east as the Klamath region. This means that five counties are included, listed alphabetically: Curry, Douglas, Jackson, Josephine, and Klamath. To be honest, I have strayed over the line a little here and there to include areas that are not, strictly speaking, within the borders of those counties, but are too good to leave out.

1

Gulls at Harris Beach State Park

1   The Best of the Coast
Boardman State Park (and redwoods, too)

I believe the coastline of Southern Oregon is as beautiful as any coastline anywhere, and **Samuel H. Boardman State Park** is the centerpiece.

Boardman was the first superintendent of the Oregon State Parks, and is considered to be the "father" of the state parks. He, too, must have felt that this part of the coast is outstanding, because he originally proposed that it should become a national park. However, national park status did not come to pass, apparently because of local opposition, mostly from grazing interests.

Harris Beach State Park, which is a mile north of Brookings, shares the coastal beauty of Boardman State Park. It has a sheltered beach and a campground. As a result, it is

---

OPPOSITE PAGE: Samuel H. Boardman State Park

extremely popular, and may be crowded at times when other places, just a little further north, are less populated. Along the roadside in the park, and in fact almost anywhere along the coast, look for the spectacular spikes of foxglove. Foxglove is an introduced plant from Europe, but it now grows widely in the wild in the northwest.

Boardman State Park officially begins 3 miles north of Brookings and extends for the next nine miles, with eleven marked viewpoints. Two of these, **Lone Ranch,** and

Cosmos at Azalea Park

Rhododendron at Azalea Park

Salal

Western azalea

Whalehead (steep road), have beach access and picnicking. The others don't have direct beach access, but all have spectacular views. For those who are so inclined, the viewpoints provide connections to the Oregon Coastal Trail.

Every viewpoint is worth a stop, to admire this most sensational of all coasts, but two are especially noteworthy: Natural Bridges and Arch Rock. At the **Natural Bridges** parking area, 10.6 miles north of Brookings, there is a paved barrier-free trail leading to a viewpoint directly above the double arches, in only a hundred yards or so. **Arch Rock,** 11.8 miles north of Brookings, may be the most-visited viewpoint of all. There is a large parking area, with picnic tables, restrooms, and a delightful paved barrier-free trail perhaps a quarter-mile long, that leads through a forest of Sitka spruce to the edge of the cliffs.

There's more. About 18 miles north of Brookings is the broad, sweeping beach of **Pistol River State Park.** Pistol River allegedly got its name because someone lost a pistol

Arch Rock

here in the 1850s. Whatever the source of the name, the beach has a lonely quality that seems to speak of the isolated nature of this part of Oregon.

A short distance north of Pistol River State Park is **Cape Sebastian,** arguably the most sensational viewpoint on the entire coast. The access road is paved but steep, and is not considered suitable for trailers. There are two parking lots; the farther one, called the "South Parking Lot" is the better one. Here, the small parking lot sits directly on top of the crest, and you can see for 40 or 50 miles in both directions up the coast. The only suitable word for it is "breathtaking."

Brookings is the starting point not only for Boardman State Park, but also for a side trip up the **Chetco River.** Take the North Bank Road. It is only 0.2 mile up the road to **Azalea Park** (follow signs), which is a gorgeous little city park (picnic tables and restrooms) with green lawns and paved barrier-free paths. The park has an astonishing concentration of western azaleas that are in full bloom in spring, but also has beautiful cultivated flowers that bloom during much of the year. In addition, there are rhododendrons, hazelnut shrubs, and huge Douglas-firs.

About 7.5 miles up the road is **Alfred A. Loeb State Park,** known for its large grove of "Oregon-myrtle" trees. (The same species of tree grows in California and is called "California-laurel"; in Oregon it is often known as "Oregon-myrtle.") Some of these trees are 200 years old, and are as much as six feet in diameter. Their natural way of growing causes the trees to divide into multiple trunks close to the ground, so the huge diameter of the trunk as measured at the ground becomes many trunks, each a foot or so in diameter.

About a half-mile up the road from Loeb State Park is the **Redwood Nature Trail.** (A Northwest Forest Pass, available from U. S. Forest Service ranger stations, is required for parking at the trailhead.) The trail is about a mile and a half round trip, and rises up the hill, with many switchbacks. This is one of the most northerly redwood groves in existence, and is definitely worth the effort.

The forest is dense and primeval-looking. The understory consists of ferns, salal, and huckleberry, with a carpet of oxalis in many places. Some of the redwoods are huge, up to 12 feet in diameter, although there are larger ones in California. The world's largest, in Jedediah Smith State Park, measures 25 feet in diameter. Douglas-firs can also be large, and almost as tall as redwoods. The "world champion" Douglas-fir is 13 ½ feet in diameter, and is located in Olympic National Park.

Samuel H. Boardman State Park

"Oregon-myrtle" at Loeb State Park

Foxglove

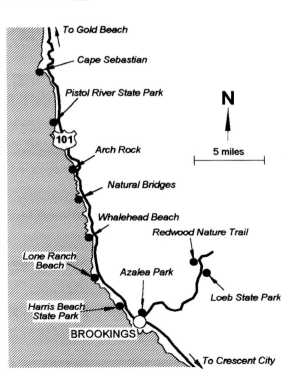

Ox-eye daisies growing wild at coast near Port Orford

2   Gold Beach to Bandon

An uncrowded coastline

Gold Beach got its name by a simple process: gold was discovered there in the beach sands, in the 1850s. Actually, gold was found on the beaches in many places in Southern Oregon at about the same time. Today, Gold Beach is best known for its fishing, and for the jet-boat trips up the Rogue River.

Twenty-eight miles up the coast is **Port Orford,** which is considered to be one of the more remote places on the coast. Yet this is part of its charm, at least for visitors, and perhaps for the residents. The town is perched on the cliffs above its harbor, which is so exposed to the ocean that boats must be hoisted onto the pier when not in use, to protect them from wave action. Ox-eye daisies and sweet peas are scattered on the clifftops.

The view to the south from Port Orford is unobstructed all the way to **Humbug Mountain,** which has an attractive state park campground at its base. When coming from the

OPPOSITE PAGE: View of Beach from Coquille Point

south, the highway has to climb inland and go around the mountain, to avoid the cliffs that plunge into the sea. Then, as the road finds its way back to the coast, it runs next to a delightful brook that never seems to lack for water no matter what the season.

The headlands above Port Orford until the 1960s were the site of a Coast Guard station. Today, the headlands have been made into a state park, called **Port Orford Heads State Park.** Three trails radiate from the station out to the headlands, the longest of which is about a mile, round-trip. The one called "Headland Trail," provides magnificent views of the ocean and coastline. To get to the park, turn west off US 101 onto 9th Street, and follow signs.

Once you leave Port Orford, for a hundred miles to the north the coast is not visible from US 101, except at one point near Umpqua Lighthouse State Park, where there is a viewpoint of the ocean. It is necessary to get off US 101 and explore to the west, to discover what a magnificent section of coast this is.

The first opportunity is the turnoff to **Cape Blanco State Park,** about four miles north of Port Orford. It is about 5 miles to the cape, past cranberry bogs. The road is lined with

Perennial sweet pea

Seaside daisy

Sanderling

Hedge morning-glory

blackberry and fire-weed, and also with European gorse, which most people probably could do without. But in May, the roadsides and fields are filled with the most incredible display of Douglas iris that it has ever been my fortune to see. Also, at the cape itself, there are abundant clumps of iris.

Cape Blanco is the westernmost point in Oregon. There is a lighthouse, open for tours in summer. But the main attraction, in this exposed location,

Beach strawberry

are the heart-stopping views to north and south. The wildflowers that carpet the headlands in spring and summer add to the charm.

The campsites in the state park are essentially carved out of the dense thickets of Sitka spruce, huckleberries, and salal. Windy days are frequent on this exposed headland, but the snug sites are well protected. On a sunny day, when the wind isn't blowing, it's a bit of heaven.

About four miles north of the Cape Blanco turnoff is the side road that leads to **Boice Cope County Park.** It's about 3.5 miles to the park, and it's worth the trip, because the campground sits directly on top of the bluffs overlooking **Floras Lake,**

Douglas iris

11

Floras Lake

and on out to sea. Here is one place where you can sit in your campsite and watch the sun set into the Pacific.

The southern shore of Floras Lake is a state park, but it is undeveloped and difficult of access. The county park side, in addition to having a beautiful overlook, is a mecca for windsurfers. Thus, the park can be jammed on weekends.

For non-windsurfers, there is a trail only about a half-mile long to the wide and untrammeled beach. Yet, even here there are restrictions, because the beach is also attractive to nesting snowy plovers. About a one-mile stretch of the beach is closed from March 15 to September 15, but both north and south of the closed area are miles of seemingly deserted coast.

In 1910, some folks thought Floras Lake could be turned into a seaport, by digging a canal to the ocean. The town of Lakeport was founded, about where the county park now is located, and at one time had 400 residents. But it was then learned that the canal would have the effect of draining the lake into the ocean, and Lakeport was abandoned.

Even though the coast highway in this region does not provide much in the way of ocean views, there is a nice visual dividend available in May, provided one is alert. Wild rhododendrons grow in the forest, and the lovely rose-colored blooms often peek from the forest edges.

Many people stick to US 101 when passing through Bandon, little suspecting what a gorgeous coastline lies less than a mile to the west. In Bandon, turn west on Eleventh Street SW, and go 0.8 mile to Coquille Point. From here, if you go south on Beach Loop Drive, there are five scenic overlooks. **Coquille Point**, owned and developed by the U.S. Fish and Wildlife Service, is the first one. It has a parking area, restrooms, a delightful paved trail leading around the point, with many interpretive signs and benches, and stairways to the beach. The view from the point is one of the finest on the coast.

Wildflowers cover the edges of the headlands, including seaside daisies, angelica, hedge morning glory, clover, beach strawberries, and wild radish. Brown pelicans can be seen flying by in summer, and in spring common murres, gulls, and cormorants nest on the offshore rocks. In some years, as many as 30,000 murres have been estimated to be nesting on these and nearby rocks. In places they can almost turn the rocks black, the birds are so dense.

If you are traveling south, there are four more viewpoints in the next three miles. **Face Rock Wayside** (0.5 mile south) and **Bandon State Park** (2.1 miles south) are two of the better ones. Bandon State Park has attractively-situated picnic tables, restrooms, and beach access. At Face Rock, there is a large offshore island that has a distinct human profile to it. In winter, here is a good place to see sanderlings, that look like so many little clockwork toys chasing the edge of the surf.

Face Rock at sunset

Wildlife observation deck at Bandon Marsh

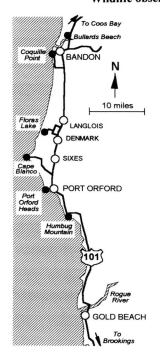

North of Bandon, just after crossing the bridge over Coquille River, **Bullards Beach State Park** is on the left, with a large campground, and a road leading out to Coquille River lighthouse. Two-tenths mile from the south edge of the Coquille River bridge is Riverside Drive. Turn west here, and it is just a short distance to **Bandon Marsh National Wildlife Refuge,** where the Fish and Wildlife Service has constructed a boardwalk and viewing deck. Bandon Marsh may look like just so much mudflats, but it is one of the principal locations on the Oregon Coast for migrating shorebirds.

OPPOSITE PAGE: Douglas iris at Cape Blanco

14

At Cape Arago

3   Cape Arago and Coos Bay

Beautiful coast, wonderful gardens

Coos Bay and North Bend together have about 25,000 population, making this region the most citified spot on the Oregon coast. The region also has some of the loveliest places on the Oregon coast.

The jewel in the crown is **Shore Acres State Park.** To get there, leave US 101 in either Coos Bay or North Bend where the signs say "State Parks," and follow the signs through Charleston, first to Sunset Bay State Park, and then to Shore Acres. It is 11 or 12 miles to Shore Acres, depending upon your departure point.

The magnificent gardens at this park are what remains of the three-story "summer home" constructed here by lumber baron Louis J. Simpson in 1914. In 1921 the house was destroyed by fire, but in 1927 Simpson began to rebuild it. The stock market crash of 1929 terminated the construction work, and in 1948 the partially completed house was torn down.

OPPOSITE PAGE: Silver Falls, at Golden and Silver Falls State Park

Shore Acres

The "summer house" was located on the cliffs where the observation building now stands. The view of the waves on the rocks below is impressive, but it is the gardens that attract most of the visitors. These are beautifully maintained by the state parks service, and there is something in bloom almost the entire year. Next to the formal gardens is a small oriental garden, and a separate rose garden is nearby. Trails lead from the gardens along the edges of the cliffs for even more spectacular ocean views.

A mile or so before coming to Shore Acres is **Sunset Bay State Park**. This delightful park is enormously popular, and the campground is often full. A part of the attraction is Sunset Bay itself, which is an attractive cove with a protected beach, gentle waves, green lawns, and picnic tables.

Cape Arago State Park is a mile or so beyond Shore Acres, and is the end of the road. (Arago is pronounced AIR-ah-go.) There are picnic tables, parking, restrooms, and sensational views. Simpson Reef lies just offshore and can have an astonishing population of sea lions.

Bastendorf Beach County Park is about 2 miles back down the road toward Charleston. This is another popular park with a high-quality campground, and a protected beach of its own. From the park, one can observe huge ocean-going ships moving up the channel toward Coos Bay. Watching the sunset from the beach is a nightly ritual. (Provided it's not foggy, of course.)

Charleston is a charming little port town, with boats galore, shops, and restaurants. It is situated where South Slough meets the main part of Coos Bay itself. Farther up South Slough is the **South Slough National Estuarine Research Reserve.** To get to the reserve, take Seven Devils Road out of Charleston, and go about 4.5 miles south from town to the visitor center. (The name "Seven Devils" reportedly comes from the rough nature of the coastal area south of Cape Arago, with its profusion of ridges and ravines.)

Several trails originate at the visitor center. The shortest is the "Ten-Minute Trail," which makes a short loop below the center, and has interpretive signs. A somewhat longer hike is down the "Hidden Creek Trail" or the "Big Cedar Trail" to the slough, then over to the "Sloughside Pilings," and back up the "Timber Trail." A map of the trails is available free at the visitor center. The Big Cedar Trail is barrier-free. Access to this trail can be arranged through the visitor center for those who can't hike the regular trails.

The trails lead down through dense undergrowth, which mostly consists of salal and huckleberry, with a few rhododendrons. Wrentits and winter wrens can be heard calling, because thick undergrowth is where they live. At the bottom of the trail there is a large viewing platform that gives a view of the estuary.

The better views come later. From the viewing platform, the "Tunnel Trail" (called that, because of the tunnels through the undergrowth) leads to more viewing platforms, and

Sunset at Bastendorf Beach

ends on the top of an old dike ("Sloughside Pilings") that offers great views in all directions. I saw a river otter in the slough when I was there.

The decaying pilings here are remnants of an old logging railroad that led at one time up the slough. The pilings remind us that most of the South Slough area was logged or farmed beginning in 1850 and extending into the middle of the 20th century. The fact that the area looks almost pristine today shows the tremendous recuperative power of nature, when it is given the chance.

A side excursion from Coos Bay to **Golden and Silver Falls State Park** is worth the trip. On the south side of Coos Bay, turn east off US 101 onto the road to Allegany. The park is 9.6 miles beyond Allegany, and 24 miles from Coos Bay. The road is paved except for the last 5 miles, which is gravel. The two falls are in different canyons, and the trail to each is about ¼ mile in length.

Silver Falls (see photo on page 16) is an unusual fall because the water spreads over a dome-like structure at the top before falling 80 feet to the bottom. It doesn't at all resemble the falls at the popular Silver Falls State Park, near Salem. Golden Falls is more conventional in appearance and is higher -- 125 to 150 feet. Since one of the falls is named "silver," it is usually assumed that the other must be called that because it is "golden" in color. But no. It is named after Dr. C.B. Golden.

South Slough, at Sloughside Pilings

Golden Falls

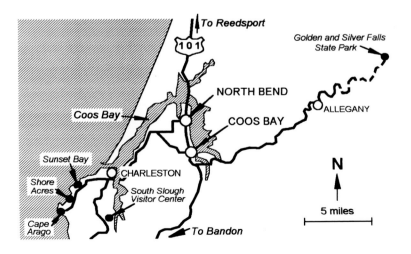

21

4 A Magnificent Estuary
Rivers, dunes, and lakes

There are several winding estuaries along the Oregon coast, each of them a drowned river valley that penetrates into the Coast Range. Next to the estuary of the mighty Columbia River, I think the most dramatic one is the Umpqua River, which extends from Winchester Bay into the mountains for 25 miles, to Scottsburg. (The Columbia estuary, by contrast, extends inland for 130 miles.)

Scottsburg was founded in 1850, and for two years prospered as a seaport, because the valley of the Umpqua River gave access to the interior and to the gold mines. However, it was soon superseded by Crescent City, which gave better access to the mines. Today, it is hard to conjure up a vision of ocean-going vessels laboring their way up the river to Scottsburg.

Highway 38 runs close to the estuary for miles. In places, human habitations are not visible, and the forested mountains come directly down to the water, giving a wild, remote feeling.

The feeling of wildness is enhanced by the presence of an area about three miles east of Reedsport, on OR 38, where Roosevelt elk can be seen. This is the **Dean Creek Elk Viewing Area,** managed by the Bureau of Land Management. The elk are usually out in the open, and the last time we were there we counted 75. They have become so accustomed to cars, and to people stopping to look, that they pay scarcely any attention. They choose to remain in this location probably because they know they are safe, and because there is plenty of food available.

On one occasion, in fall, we were watching the elk. To one side was a large male with a great set of antlers, grazing in the middle of his harem. A hundred yards away another male was grazing, all alone. His antlers, though impressive, were not as large as those of the first elk.

OPPOSITE PAGE:
   Painted lady butterfly, at
   Butterfly Pavilion

AT RIGHT:
   Umpqua River Estuary

Roosevelt elk at Dean Creek Viewing Area

We wondered whether, in their previous encounters, the dominance of one over the other had already been established, so that one male had all the available females, and the smaller one, none.

We observed that, in their grazing, the two were slowly coming closer to each other. We wondered what would happen if the "comfort distance" between the two became too small. Suddenly, the large elk lifted his head, looked at the smaller one, and then assumed a threatening posture, moving three steps forward.

The smaller elk paid no attention, but continued grazing. However, all the other elk in view, including those at a distance, stopped grazing, lifted their heads and stood as if at attention, watching the two males.

Nothing happened. The smaller elk continued to graze as if he was unaware of his surroundings, and we noticed that he was the *only* elk that was not standing at attention. At this point the larger elk, apparently satisfied that the smaller elk knew his place, turned around and laid down. Instantly, all the heads that had been lifted to watch, dropped to the ground to graze.

The mouth of the Umpqua River occupies the geographical center of the **Oregon Dunes National Recreation Area.** Sand dunes occur on about half of the Oregon coast, but the most dramatic ones are in the 54-mile section where the National Recreation Area is located, from Coos Bay to Florence.

The Umpqua River has created a passage through the dunes, and goes all the way to the ocean. In other locations, where the smaller rivers lacked sufficient power, the dunes blocked their access to the sea and freshwater lakes were created. These lakes, such as Tahkenitch Lake and Clear Lake, are some of the beautiful natural features of the Oregon coast. US 101 runs directly on the shore of Clear Lake, and the view is lovely, except for a concrete safety barrier next to the road.

There is something about dunes that fascinates people. Of course, many people like them because they can ride their off-road vehicles through the dunes, and many campgrounds in the area cater to those folks. Others appreciate them for their own beauty, and the area has been divided into zones to cater to each type.

What most people don't know is that the dunes look a lot different today than they did 100 to 150 years ago, or even 30 years ago. In 1889, the first comprehensive survey of the area described the country as almost entirely burned over.

A more recent change has to do with extensive plantings, to prevent sand from drifting across highways, or from destroying houses, which apparently has happened occasionally. The first attempts involved the introduction of European beach grass to stabilize the dunes. Later stabilization efforts have involved a succession of plantings -- first, the beach grass, then another introduced plant, Scotch broom (considered today to be a noxious weed), and finally, shore pines. The theory was that the Scotch broom would eventually die under the shade of the growing pines, leaving the pines as the dominant vegetation.

One result of human activity, whether from fire suppression or from dune stabilization, is that areas that were open and meadowy as recently as 30 years ago now consist of dense

Oregon Dunes from dunes overlook

thickets of shore pine, Sitka spruce, western wax myrtle, and evergreen huckleberry. However, visitors today don't seem to worry about the past, and continue to throng to the Oregon Dunes, either for their solemn beauty, or for mechanized recreation.

Fifteen miles up the Umpqua River highway (OR 38) is the turnoff to **Loon Lake.** It is 7 miles up the paved side road to Loon Lake itself. The lake was created by a huge landslide that occurred more than a thousand years ago. The canyon bottom is strewn with the gigantic boulders from the slide, and the entrance road to Loon Lake snakes between them.

There is an excellent campground and a well-developed beach at the lake. As a result, the lake is popular and crowded on summer weekends. A delightful trail, partly paved, leads along the western shore of the lake, and, in about a half-mile comes to a small waterfall. The trail is through apparently undisturbed forest, with large firs, ferns, and redwood sorrel.

Another kind of wildlife exists further up OR 38, just a mile or so west of Elkton, at the **Butterfly Pavilion** of the Elkton Community Education Center. Monarch and painted lady butterflies can be watched at close range in a walk-in enclosure. In an adjacent room, classes of school children can observe the process whereby monarch larvae turn into chrysalises, and then into adult butterflies

Loon Lake in autumn

Redwood sorrel

Trail next to Loon Lake

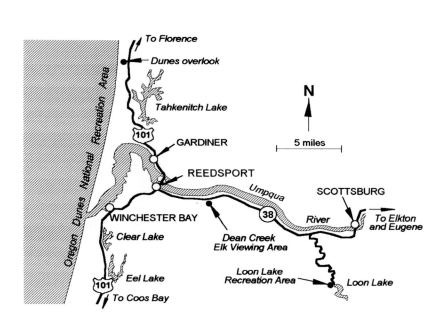

5 Thundering Waters

Exploring the North Umpqua

It is said that the Indian word *umpqua* means "thundering waters," which certainly seems appropriate for the waterfalls and rapids of the North Umpqua River. But it is also said that *umpqua* might mean "the sound the water makes," or "across the water," or "one is satisfied." No matter. All these names work fine for me, and all of them describe the North Umpqua.

In my view, the **North Umpqua River** is one of the most scenic rivers anywhere. For more than 40 miles, State Highway 138 runs next to the river, almost always in sight of its white rapids and great green pools. Most of this section has been formally designated as a Wild and Scenic River. The river is a great draw for anglers, and hardly any highway has more turnouts and waysides, to accommodate them.

And of course the river attracts rafters and kayakers. I'm not a rafter or kayaker myself, but my literature tells me that the river abounds in Class III rapids. Class III rapids, I am told, are:

> Rapids with high, irregular waves often capable of swamping an open canoe. Narrow passages may require complex maneuvering and scouting from shore.

There are even a couple of Class IV and Class V rapids, with suitably scary descriptions, which may or may not appeal to rafters. But, to the non-rafter, what all this means is that the North Umpqua is one gorgeous river, truly meriting the name "thundering waters."

Nine campgrounds are situated along the highway, some of them directly on the river. One of these, **Susan Creek Recreation Site** (29.5 miles from Roseburg) has been described by the Bureau of Land Management as a "prized recreation site." All of the campsites in this campground are paved, and have

---

OPPOSITE PAGE:
Toketee Falls

Watson Falls

Tiger Lily

Hermit thrush

been designed for disabled access. Above all, they are beautifully situated in a magnificent forest.

Once, as I was sitting in a campsite there, a rufous hummingbird flew up directly in front of my face, checking me out. Then it dropped down to the red sleeves of my jacket, and carefully investigated each fold, in case one of them happened to contain nectar. To complete the scene, a hermit thrush sang its ethereal song from some hidden spot in the forest.

But the waterfalls are the prize attractions of the area. Seven of them lie close to the route of Highway 138. One of these, Watson Falls, 272 feet high, is the fourth highest waterfall in Oregon. Another, Toketee Falls, is a double fall totaling 160 feet, and it has a graceful beauty that is equal to any fall, anywhere.

Here are the waterfalls, with the mileage from Roseburg shown in each case. An excellent time to visit them is in June, when there is plenty of water, and wildflowers are at their peak.

Deadline Falls. Turn south on Swiftwater Road, 22.0 miles from Roseburg, cross the bridge, and then turn left into the parking lot. It is about 0.3 mile on a wheelchair-accessible trail to the overlook, through magnificent old-growth forest.

As waterfalls go, this is probably the least impressive of the lot, because it is only ten feet high or so. But it is right on the main river, so it has a lot of power. Furthermore, it has been designated as a Watchable Wildlife site, because in the summer you can see salmon and steelhead attempting to jump the falls. Along the trail and at the viewpoint, look for twinflower and Queen Anne's lace in spring. Also, look for poison oak. Tiger lilies lurk in shady wet sites. As you continue east on Highway 138, the falls are briefly visible from the highway, the only waterfall along the route that can be seen from the highway itself.

Susan Creek Falls. The entrance to the parking lot is on north side of highway, 29.2 miles from Roseburg, directly opposite Susan Creek Day-use Area. It is a hike of about 0.8

mile to the falls. The trail is designed to be wheelchair-accessible, although it may be somewhat steep for wheelchairs in a couple of places.

The trail passes through mature forest, consisting mostly of Douglas-fir, dogwood, hazelnut, bigleaf and vine maples, salal, and, of course, poison oak. Checkermallow blooms in sunny spots, in spring.

This is Swainson's thrush and winter wren country. Swainson's thrushes are seldom seen, but their mysterious, upward-ascending flute-like whistle is heard often in the forest. Winter wrens are more likely to show themselves, leaping energetically about, with their stubby tails held upright. Their songs are heard frequently in thick, damp undergrowth such as on the Susan Creek Falls trail.

The winter wren's song has an almost out-ot-this-world quality, sounding much like a rapid high-pitched tinkling of tiny bells. It typically goes on so long that you wonder how such a tiny body can hold so much breath. When not singing, the birds bustle about in the underbrush, generally out of sight, and give a frequently repeated call note -- *chik! chik-chik! chik-chik!*

Fall Creek Falls. The trail signs for this destination are a bit confusing. The main display board says it is 0.9 mile, but as soon as you cross the first bridge, it says ½ mile. I'd bet on 0.9 mile being closer to the truth, with an elevation gain of about 200 feet. The parking lot is 32.6 miles from Roseburg.

Winter wren

Checkermallow

There's only one word for this trail: delightful. It is in a beautiful canyon, with a lovely stream nearby, with lots of ferns, redwood sorrel, salal, and old growth. The falls are impressive, and descend in a double fall, one of about 30 feet and the other 50 feet.

Toketee Falls. If you only have time for one fall, this is it. The turnoff to the falls comes at 59.0 miles from Roseburg. After turning, you go 0.2 mile, turn left, cross the bridge, and immediately turn left again into the parking area next to the huge pipe made of redwood staves. The pipe has many spouting leaks, and carries a huge volume of water from Toketee Lake to a power plant below.

Rhododendron

Bunchberry dogwood

The trail is only 0.4 mile, but has 97 steps up and 127 down. (That's what the trail sign says, and I counted them. The sign is right.) The trail is suspended on the side of the canyon, and passes through delightful forest, including rhododendrons, vine maple, and dogwood. It leads to a beautifully constructed viewing platform that seems to be suspended in mid-air, and gives you a view directly into the falls.

This is a double fall, on the North Umpqua River itself, and thus has an impressive volume of water. It makes you wonder what it would be like if it weren't for the huge amount of water that goes through that redwood pipe, bypassing the falls. The upper fall goes into a bowl suspended halfway up the cliff, and the lower fall spills out of the bowl and plunges 80 feet into a large green pool. There are basalt columnar formations on both sides, giving an artistic effect that would make a landscape architect proud.

Watson Falls. The parking lot is 61.3 miles from Roseburg. Not only does the parking lot have picnic tables nicely situated next to the creek, it also has a handsome collection of rhododendrons around its edges, that come into bloom in mid-June.

Watson Falls is the highest of the lot, and is an impressive straight drop from the cliff edge. It is visible from the parking lot, but the view is much more satisfying up higher. It is about 0.4 mile to a close-up view point, with a fair amount of climbing. The forest through which the trail leads is an unusually attractive one, and runs in places close to the creek. There are rhododendron, vine maple, thimbleberry, and Oregon grape. This, too, is Winter Wren country, and their tinkling songs can frequently be heard in the canyon.

Whitehorse Falls (66.1 miles from Roseburg) and **Clearwater Falls** (69.7 miles from Roseburg) seem rather insignificant after viewing the falls already described, but they are easy to access, and worth a visit. A nice bonus, when we were at Clearwater Falls, was the presence of a resident American dipper, who asserted his ownership of the territory by occupying, in turn, every rock or log below the falls. Another bonus was the discovery of bunchberry dogwood plants, lying flat on the ground, with their tiny white flowers glowing in the shade. Just why this plant isn't called Canadian dogwood, after its scientific name, *Cornus canadensis,* is not clear to me.

The forest beyond Clearwater Falls is different from that at the lower elevations, and consists mostly of lodgepole pines. Lodgepoles generally do not make the most beautiful forest in the world, but an attractive feature of the region is the spreading phlox and tiny blue lupine that covers the edges of the road in places.

Diamond Lake lies in the upper reaches of the North Umpqua drainage, about 80 miles from Roseburg. The lake is legendary for its beauty, and has a huge, highly developed campground along its east shore. The pointy Mount Thielsen rises above the lake, causing one to ask the question: "Do people really climb that thing?" People do, but not easily.

Diamond Lake, and Mount Thielsen

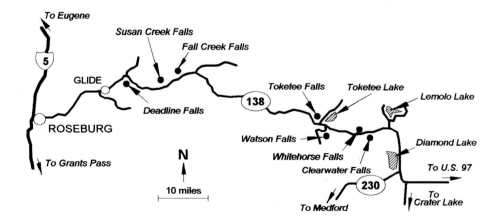

6 Lower Rogue
Hellgate, Rainie Falls, and Illahe

The "Lower Rogue" is generally thought to begin at Hellgate, and from there runs through a narrow canyon to the coast at Gold Beach. This section of the river is what many people mean, when they refer to the "Rogue River." For much of this distance, the river consists of rapids, and is a whitewater rafter's paradise. From Grave Creek, where the major whitewater section begins, to Illahe, where it ends, the river is touched by only one road -- a gravel one -- at Marial.

From Illahe to the coast, the river is tamer than in the sections upstream, and jet boats make regular runs from Gold Beach. In fact, there is a jet boat "whitewater" trip that runs all the way to Blossom Bar, 10 miles upstream from Illahe. (Blossom Bar is a difficult Class IV rapid, and is not negotiable by the jet boats.)

To get to Grave Creek, where the roadless part of the river begins, take Exit 61 from I-5 north of Grants Pass, and follow the high standard road through Merlin and Galice (called the Merlin-Galice Road). It is about 23 miles to the **Grave Creek Bridge.** Near the bridge is **Grave Creek Landing,** where many whitewater enthusiasts put into the river.

From there, you can either return to I-5 and come out near Wolf Creek, or you can take

the steep, narrow, partly gravel road that begins at the north end of the bridge and goes all the way to the coast. From Grave Creek Bridge to Gold Beach it is about 100 miles of slow, tedious driving. The road may be closed in the winter by snow.

An alternative route is to go north on I-5 to Exit 80, for Glendale. As you enter Glendale, where the sign says, "Welcome to Glendale," turn right on the truck route, cross a bridge, and immediately turn left on Road 27, called Reuben Road. From there, it is about 12 miles to Riffle Creek Junction, where you turn left on Road 32-7-19.3 (narrow, but paved) and go 8.0 miles to the junction with the road coming up from

OPPOSITE PAGE:
  Cream fawn lily on trail
  to Rainie Falls

AT RIGHT:
  Rogue River below Grave Creek

Grave Creek Bridge (see above). **If you attempt to drive to the coast by either route, make sure you have a full tank of gas.**

On the route from I-5 through Merlin to the Grave Creek Bridge, you pass **Hellgate Canyon,** about 6 miles from Merlin. Trips through Hellgate are major features of local jet-boat and rafting excursions. There is an overlook next to the road from which you can peer (sort of) down into Hellgate. In early spring, lupine, long-leaved storksbill, and seep-spring monkeyflower decorate the cliffs, especially where there are springs and other wet places.

At the south end of Grave Creek Bridge there is a trailhead and roadside parking for the trail to **Rainie Falls.** The falls are named for J.N. Rainey, who lived near the falls in the

Long-beaked storksbill

Seep-spring monkeyflower

Spring gold

Larkspur

early part of the 20th century. Your guess is as good as mine, as to how the name got from "Rainey" to "Rainie."

Rainie Falls

The trail to Rainie Falls is about two miles in length, and ends at the falls. On the opposite side of the canyon is the Rogue River Trail, which goes all the way to Illahe.

The trail to Rainie Falls is very popular, and rightly so. Since it is on the shady side of the canyon, the forest is lusher than on the other side, and is packed with wildflowers in early spring. Fawn lilies line the trail, sometimes abundantly. There also are shooting stars, spring gold, saxifrage, larkspur, and pink redwood sorrel.

The trail is considered easy by most persons, although there are several ups and downs, some of them steep. In places, the trail consists of narrow rocky ledges that have literally been hacked out of the cliffs. It is not a place for small children.

The falls themselves don't look like a classic waterfall, but instead consist of a giant rapid, with a drop of 10 to 15 feet. This is one of the most severe rapids on the Rogue River, and is considered to be Class V, according to *The Rogue River Guide*.

As already described, the only road that touches the river between Grave Creek Bridge and Illahe is the one to Marial. After the junction between the road from Grave Creek Landing and Road 32-7-19.3, mentioned above, the road number becomes 32-8-31 (paved). Take this road in the direction of the coast, and, after 4.8 miles take the road (number 32-9-14.2) on the left that leads to Rogue River Ranch. It is 13.6 miles to the ranch, on a road that is partly paved and partly gravel.

Rogue River Ranch is managed by the Bureau of Land Management as an historical site, and is a delightful green spot with red buildings next to the confluence of Mule Creek and the Rogue River. The ranch area was first settled more than 100 years ago, and was the center of social life for the 75 to 100 people living in the area. The location was named "Marial" after the daughter of the early settlers. The buildings first acquired their red color in 1956.

In spring, the road to **Marial** is lined with wildflowers, including fawn lilies, common madia, paintbrush, larkspur, blue dicks, broadleaf stonecrop, California poppies, pussy ears, Douglas iris, and yellow-leaved iris. In the lower sections of the road, close to the river, it seems that iris plants are everywhere, ranging in color from white, to yellow, to magenta.

When you depart from Marial, you have to go 13.6 miles back up the road you came down. From the junction of Roads 32-8-31 and 32-9-14.2, it is about 46 miles to Illahe, where you join the Rogue River again. Follow signs saying "Coast."

In the 1860s, the area around **Illahe** attracted settlers, especially because of the nearby meadows at Big Bend. A major battle was fought here between the army and the Rogue River Indians, in 1856. Close by is Foster Bar, the major takeout point on the lower river for rafters.

Common madia

Golden iris

Douglas iris

Broadleaf stonecrop

Yellow-leaved iris in Lower Rogue River Canyon

From Illahe it is 30 miles downriver, on paved (but sometimes rough) road, to the coast at Gold Beach, with only occasional views of the Rogue River. In May, there can be astonishing numbers of golden iris on the roadsides and in the forest.

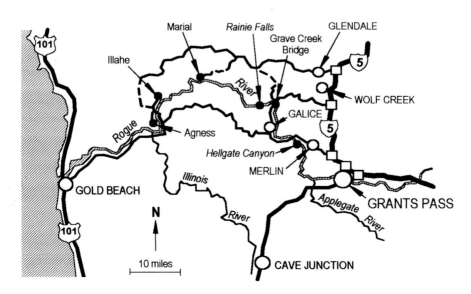

The Chateau and the Chalet

7 Cave Country
Plus cobra lilies and Bolan Lake

When the **Oregon Caves** first came to public attention in the 1870s, they were widely billed by newspapers as "a worthy rival to Mammoth Caves in Kentucky." This is a rather extreme claim, because the 350 miles of the Mammoth Cave system make it the largest in the world, compared to the three miles of known passageways in the Oregon Caves. Today, both the Mammoth Caves and the Oregon Caves are parts of the National Park System.

Even though they don't come close to the Mammoth Caves for magnitude, the Oregon Caves are charming, and are well decorated with the calcite formations that one expects to see in caves. Tens of thousands of people visit them every year, and in the middle of summer there can be long waits to get in. The round trip is approximately one mile, with about

---

OPPOSITE PAGE: Calcite formations in the caves

Trail from caves

500 steps involved. It is not for people in poor condition, or for small children. Also, visitors are warned about bumping their heads on rock outcroppings.

A part of the charm of Oregon Caves is their location in the heart of the Siskiyou Mountains. The caves are in a narrow canyon full of old-growth forest, and several nature trails run through the area. In spring, wildflowers such as wild roses and Columbia windflowers bloom. The haunting songs of hermit thrushes are heard in the forest, and Steller's jays shout their *shek-shek-shek-shek!* as they fly from one tree to another. If one does no more than to walk the trail through the forest from the caves back to the visitor center, it can be a rewarding experience.

In the canyon next to the caves a small village has been constructed, consisting principally of two historic buildings, the Chalet and the Chateau. The canyon is so narrow and constricted that parking has had to be provided about 900 feet back down the road, and most visitors walk the last 900 feet to get to the caverns. Overnight guests are allowed to park in the village.

The Chalet, which now serves as the visitor center, was constructed in 1923 (rebuilt in 1941), and the six-story Chateau, which has rental rooms and a restaurant, was finished in 1934. The Chateau is tucked into the canyon is such a way that it appears to be only two stories high from the front, but is six stories high when viewed from the canyon below.

Grayback interpretive trail

Calypso orchid

Woodland phlox

California ground-cone

OPPOSITE PAGE: Steller's Jay

The creek flowing from the caves plunges directly into a pool in front of the Chateau. Both the Chalet and Chateau came close to being destroyed in the "Christmas Flood" of 1964. Much of Oregon experienced destruction from floods at that time.

The caves lie 19 miles east of Cave Junction, via OR 46. **Grayback Campground,** maintained by the U.S. Forest Service, is 11.4 miles from Cave Junction on OR 46, and is a delightful spot, worthy of a visit on its own merits. (Visitors to the caves who are pulling trailers are urged to leave their trailers at Grayback Campground, or at the visitor center in Cave Junction.) A wheelchair-accessible trail, called the **Grayback Interpretive Trail,** has been constructed along Sucker Creek, next to the day-use area in the campground.

Siskiyou iris

Sickle-leaved onion

Long-leaved phlox

Hooker Indian pink

In spring, there are wildflowers in the campground and along the interpretive trail, such as Pacific dogwood, woodland phlox, Columbia windflower, and vanilla leaf. Two unusual flowers that might be completely overlooked in the forest litter are calypso orchid and California ground-cone. The ground-cone looks almost exactly like a pine cone sitting on the forest floor, and is a parasite on the roots of manzanita and madrone.

In the fall, the forest surrounding the campground is aglow with yellow and pink, from hazelnut, dogwood, vine maple, and bigleaf maple.

There are not many natural lakes in the Siskiyous, but **Bolan Lake** is easily accessible, and is like a small gem, situated in a forest of firs. The lake is in a small bowl, with Bolan Mountain (6269 feet) on one side and a campground on the other. A trail originates in the campground and runs along the edge of the lake.

Wildflowers such as woodland phlox, paintbrush, pussy paws, and red-flowering currant line the road to the lake in spring. Also, especially in spring, when there are snow patches still clinging to the higher mountains, the view from the road toward the high mountains in California, to the south, is magnificent.

To get to Bolan Lake, go south from Cave Junction on US 199 6.3 miles and turn east on Waldo Road, which ultimately leads to Happy Camp (and is called Happy Camp Road after crossing Takilma Road), on the Klamath River. From US 199 it is 17.0 miles on paved highway to the branch road to Bolan Lake, which is gravel, but can be traveled by ordinary cars in good weather. It is an additional 5.8 miles to the lake.

Along Waldo Road and Happy Camp Road, there can be abundant numbers of Siskiyou iris, which are pretty much

Red-flowering currant

Deltoid balsamroot

Cobra lilies (*Darlingtonia*)

restricted to the Siskiyou Mountains. Along the roadside, particularly in rocky places, look for the bright magenta flowers of long-leaved phlox, and Hooker Indian pink.

A couple of other nearby attractions are of interest. One is the **Darlingtonia Botanical Area,** and the other is the **Rough and Ready Botanical Wayside.**

"Darlingtonias" *(Darlingtonia californica)* are also known as pitcher plants, and sometimes as cobra lilies. Certainly, their specialized leaves resemble cobras, rising a foot or two from the boggy soil, each "leaf" with a hood at the top. The hoods form enclosures that trap insects, and the insects are then used by the plants as food. Cobra lilies are found in the eastern United States, but in the west occur only in northern California and southern Oregon. They are always in wet areas that are sometimes called "bogs," but are more appropriately called "fens."

A nice cobra lily fen has been developed jointly for public access by the Bureau of Land Management and the U.S. Forest Service. To get there, go 3.7 miles south of Selma on US 199, and turn west on Eight Dollar Mountain Road. It is 0.9 mile to a parking area on the left-hand side of the road.

Directly across Eight Dollar Mountain Road is a narrow paved road leading to a tiny parking area (2 spaces) intended for handicapped persons. It is a short walk (somewhat steep) up the narrow road to the handicapped parking lot, where a boardwalk begins that leads to the fen. Along the boardwalk, many wildflowers occur in spring, such as shooting stars, white violets, and blue grassnut lilies. Look, especially, for the bright magenta flowers of sickle-leaved onion.

Two miles beyond the Darlingtonia area is the Illinois River, which has been formally designated as a Wild and Scenic River. Along the shady slopes near the river, fawn lilies and white trilliums are widespread in spring.

Rough and Ready Botanical Wayside is 5.0 miles south of Cave Junction on US 199. There is a small parking area, and a trail leads through the area. It doesn't exactly qualify as a "beautiful place," and in fact is rather scraggy-looking. One might wonder why it merits a name like "botanical wayside." But the underlying geological structure consists of a rock called serpentine. Most plants don't grow well in serpentine soils (which accounts for the scraggy appearance), but there are other plants that thrive in serpentine. Thus, serpentine areas are of great botanical interest.

In spring, the wayside supports a variety of wildflowers. One of the early ones is a lovely deep magenta lily-like flower called purple-eyed grass, grass-widows, or satin-flower. Also, look for pussy ears, larkspur, deltoid balsamroot, and western wallflower.

Purple-eyed grass

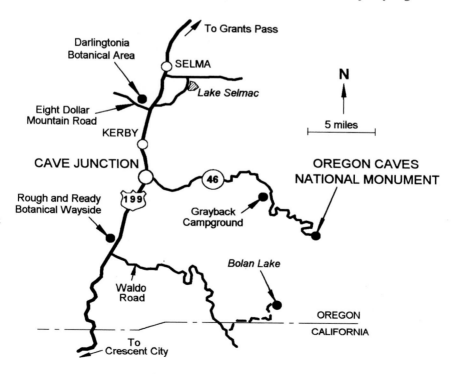

On top of Lower Table Rock, in April

8 Table Rocks
Gardens in the sky

The Table Rocks are highly visible landmarks in the Rogue Valley, and seem more appropriate to the deserts of the southwest than to Oregon. They are often referred to as "islands in the sky," a descriptive term that seems just right.

A public trail to Upper Table Rock was created in the 1970s, and to Lower Table Rock in the 1980s. In both cases, the trails came into being because of the efforts of local citizen groups, and because of land acquisitions by The Nature Conservancy (TNC). Most of the land was already owned by the Bureau of Land Management (BLM), and today the trails are managed cooperatively by TNC, BLM, and Rogue River Ranch.

The rocks are beloved by Rogue Valley residents, and an estimated 10,000 people climb them every year. The hikes are classed as moderate, ranging from 2 miles to 3 miles (round trip), with an elevation gain in each case of 700 to 800 feet. April is the most popular month, because this is when most of the flowers are out, and when the birds are most active.

OPPOSITE PAGE:
  Henderson fawn lilies

To get to the rocks from Medford, go north on OR 62 5.8 miles to Antelope Road, and turn west. Go 1.8 miles on Antelope Road to Table Rock Road and turn right (north). To get to **Upper Table Rock,** turn right (east) on Modoc Road, which is 1.8 miles north of Antelope Road, and follow signs to the parking lot. To get to **Lower Table Rock,** continue on Table Rock Road to Wheeler Road (4.2 miles from Antelope Road). Turn left (west) on Wheeler Road and follow signs to the parking lot.

Upper Table Rock is indeed slightly higher in elevation than Lower Table Rock, at 2091 feet as opposed to 2049 feet. But it's not likely you will detect the difference. Upper Table

Henderson shooting stars

Large-flowered blue-eyed Mary

Pussy ears

Rosy plectritis ("sea-blush")

Rock actually got its name because it is more upstream along the Rogue River than is Lower Table Rock.

The two trails are rather similar, in that they lead through oak savanna and brushy ceanothus and manzanita areas at the beginning, then through denser forests of madrone and Douglas-fir, and finally onto the open tops. The trails are suitable for family groups, although children (and, perhaps, adults also) should be warned about the abundant poison oak.

Sometimes poison oak lurks in the trailside grass, almost invisible, and other times the branches actually reach out into the trail. In spring the leaves are reddish, in summer they are green, and in fall they are red again. But they always show a characteristic 3-leaved pattern, causing people to say, "Leaves in three, leave it be."

Poison oak in autumn

At Lower Table Rock, the first part of the trail is well graded, and easy. Toward the top there are steep stretches, and rocky sections where you have to watch your step.

At the bottom of either trail, in the open country, meadowlarks hold forth in the spring, with their lovely flutelike songs. In the brushy and wooded areas, look for chipping sparrows and blue-gray gnatcatchers in spring. Acorn woodpeckers are highly visible any time of year. Don't be surprised if you meet a wild turkey. I once encountered one in the trail which seemed determined to have the right of way.

The trails are noted for their wildflowers in spring, such as shooting stars, rosy plectritis (sometimes called "sea-blush"), large-flowered blue-eyed Mary, buttercups, larkspur, pussy ears, common camas, hound's tongue, Henderson fawn lilies, and miner's lettuce. Don't overlook the tiny bell-shaped pinkish-white flowers of the manzanitas, which appear in March.

The views of the Rogue Valley from the tops of both rocks merit the use of a major word: *stunning.* It is possible to find a secluded perch on the edge of the vertical cliffs, and gaze at the valley below, with the great cone of Mount McLoughlin rising in the east. Turkey vultures,

Wild turkey

Miner's lettuce

red-tailed hawks, and violet-green swallows sail by at eye level. Lazuli buntings and lark sparrows may be singing.

On Lower Table Rock, if you are so inclined, you can walk across the level surface on the old abandoned air strip, clear to the opposite side, which adds about a mile each way to your trip. In spring, the surface will be almost covered with wildflowers, especially goldfields, miniature lupine, buttercups, and popcorn flowers.

On Upper Table Rock the walk across the top is shorter, and takes you to the edge of the bowl-shaped canyon in the middle. The canyon itself is off limits, but you can sit on the edge in spring and listen to the rock wrens and canyon wrens singing below.

OPPOSITE PAGE:
The Rogue Valley, from Lower Table Rock

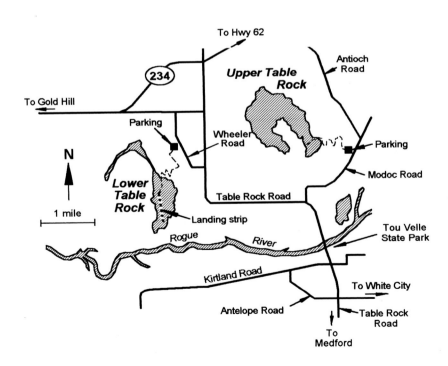

Acorn woodpecker

9 Tou Velle

Rubbing shoulders with wildlife

For many folks, **Tou Velle State Park** is primarily a great place to have a picnic. And so it is, but it is also a great place for wildlife, even though it may upon occasion teem with human life. To get there, follow the directions for the Table Rocks (previous chapter). Tou Velle State Park lies 0.8 mile north of the junction of Antelope Road and Table Rock Road, adjacent to the Rogue River.

In the fall, when salmon come up the river to spawn, the riffles alongside the exposed gravel bars in the middle of the river must seem to the fish to be ideal for spawning purposes, provided, of course, the river isn't too high. The huge fish force their way through the shallows of the gravel with their backs half way out of the water, intent upon the important business of depositing eggs.

OPPOSITE PAGE:
   Rogue River at Tou Velle State Park

Later, in winter, the same gravel bars may have a dozen or more greater yellowlegs foraging along the edges. (Are they, perhaps, seeking salmon eggs, among other things?) A greater yellowlegs, for those who don't already know, is a rather large shorebird with -- guess what -- yellow legs.

Great blue herons can be seen during most of the year, but in the early spring they begin to congregate for nesting purposes. Directly across the river from the entrance kiosk is a grove of tall cottonwood trees containing a rookery of a dozen or so nests.

Once the leaves of the trees have grown out, the nests are difficult to see, but in early March, when the herons first gather, the branches are bare and the nests are highly visible.

Greater yellowlegs

Silvery blue butterfly

Great blue herons at nest

Himalayan blackberry in autumn

Denman Marsh

People are generally accustomed to seeing a great blue heron on the ground, hunting along the shore of a lake or a marsh, but the huge birds high in the trees seem out of place.

Two other kinds of birds are closely identified with Tou Velle -- acorn woodpeckers, and tree swallows. Acorn woodpeckers live in small family groups, and each such group is tied to a so-called "granary tree." A suitable tree may be an oak, a pine, or even a telephone pole. The sides of buildings are sometimes used. In any case, a granary tree (or granary building) has typically been drilled with thousands of holes, most of them holding acorns that have been stuffed into them.

The acorns provide for a dependable food source during the winter, and a granary tree is energetically defended by a family of acorn woodpeckers. Granary trees containing as many as 20,000 acorns have been observed. In the case of Tou Velle, a granary tree -- a ponderosa pine -- is highly visible at the far end of the parking lots, near the restrooms.

Acorn woodpeckers remain in the area all year, but the tree swallows are there only in the breeding season. They begin arriving in force in March, and start competing for nesting holes. In the case of Tou Velle, some of the nesting holes are in the form of bird boxes that have been placed in the trees specifically for the purpose. There can be so many swallows around, competing for nest sites, that the sky may seem full of them.

A short nature trail begins at the far eastern end of the parking lot, that goes along the edge of the river, and then loops back through a magnificent grove of white oaks to the point of origin.   This part of the trail is perhaps a half mile round trip, and is barrier-free.   In spring, parts of the trail abound in buttercups, and a butterfly called the silvery blue can be found here, foraging in the buttercups.

If a person wants a longer walk, then one has been provided, of about 1.5 miles round trip. The starting point is the same as for the "short" walk. But, where the short walk turns away from the river, you should go straight ahead along the river, until you encounter Touvelle Road, a gravel road that was constructed for Camp White during World War II. This road is now the principal access for the **Ken Denman Wildlife Area**. At the road's point of origin, on Agate Road to the east, there is a locked gate. A key to this gate can be obtained from the wildlife area headquarters at 1495 E. Gregory Road, in Central Point.

(The observant reader will have noted the different spellings of Tou Velle, as in the state park, and Touvelle, as in Touvelle Road. I am utterly at a loss to explain the different spellings, but that is the way they are shown on the local signs.)

To continue on the "long" walk, you should turn up Touvelle Road, away from the river, and go about 0.3 mile along the road to a small dammed-up pond, where a sign says "Denman Trail," on the right-hand side of the road. The trail goes down a few steps, crosses an earthen dam that holds back the pond, and then makes a circuit back to the point of origin, climbing up on top of a low bluff at one point. Look for buttercups, rosy plectritus, blue-eyed Mary, blue dicks, and Oregon grape.

On the return, the trail passes near Denman Marsh, a rather extensive marsh with ducks and other waterbirds. In spring, listen for the odd-sounding call of the sora, a call that somewhat resembles a horse's whinny. Soras are reclusive small marsh-dwelling birds that are far more often heard than seen.

Other wildlife that might be apparent on this route are yellow-breasted chats (spring and summer) in the blackberry tangles along the river, and fox sparrows (winter) in the blackberry tangles below the bluff. The fox sparrows are likely to be very quiet, but the chats make a "song" that has been likened to a mockingbird with a sore throat. However it may be

Creeping buttercup

Blue dicks

Tree swallow   **Oregon grape**

characterized, the song is loud and repetitive, although you may never catch sight of the birds themselves.

Birds do love the blackberry tangles, although ecologists don't, because our most familiar blackberry is not a native, but is an escapee that originated in the Old World. Ecologists don't like these particular blackberries (called "Himalayan Berry") not only because they are not native, but also because they are intrusive. However, birds love them because they supply both food and shelter, and people love them because the berries are delicious.

It is claimed that there are beavers and river otters in the Rogue River, although I've never seen one there myself. Beavers are nocturnal, and thus are not likely to be seen. River otters, however, might be abroad any time of day. Even though I've not seen an otter in the Rogue River, I did see one once at Whetstone Pond, only a couple of miles away, adjacent to the Fish and Wildlife headquarters on E. Gregory Road. Otters are great overland travelers, so could get easily from one body of water to another.

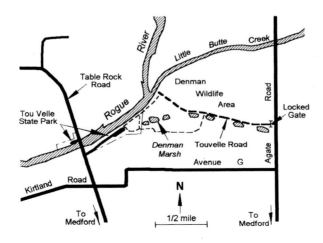

At "Rosebud Lane"

10 Bear Creek Valley

From Rosebud Lane to the Agate Desert

Bear Creek has its origins on the Siskiyou Crest below Pilot Rock and Mount Ashland, and extends from there to the Rogue River near the Table Rocks. Along the way, it passes through the most heavily populated area in Southern Oregon -- Ashland, Talent, Phoenix, Medford, and Central Point -- with about 120,000 people. There is a remarkable pathway next to the creek through much of this heavily developed area, known as the **Bear Creek Greenway**.

The Bear Creek Greenway Trail is planned to be a continuous path from Ashland to Central Point, a distance of 21 miles. Two sections were complete as of 2003: six miles from Ashland to Talent; and six miles from Medford to Central Point. These sections are paved, and are suitable for joggers, walkers, bicyclists, and wheelchairs. Dogs are required to be on

OPPOSITE PAGE: Bear Creek Greenway

61

California poppy

Purple deadnettle

leash. Ultimately, it is hoped that the trail will extend all the way from the Siskiyou crest to the Rogue River.

The management of the trail is by the cities through which it passes, or by the county, in sections that do not lie within city limits. The basic agency overseeing the trail is the Greenway Committee, composed of representatives from the communities through which it passes.

A small negative factor for the greenway is that the freeway noise of Interstate 5 is generally not very far away. In fact, along part of the trail from Medford to Central Point the freeway is right next door, and the trail is even *under* the freeway through downtown Medford. However, there are sections, especially in the Ashland-Talent stretch, where you are far enough from the freeway so you can forget about it, and just enjoy the natural surroundings.

Many kinds of wildlife live along the greenway, including muskrats, raccoons, opossums, and, reportedly, beavers. There was even a bear once, which showed up in the section near Medford, and appeared to be lost. Birds are the most prominent wildlife, and the greenway abounds with them. There also are wildflowers, although perhaps not in as much abundance as some places. At certain times of the year, the most prominent flowers may be dandelions. People usually hate dandelions, especially when they are growing in their manicured lawns. But in wild settings, I think dandelions add lovely splashes of yellow to the trailsides, and I can't help but admire them.

The greenway can be accessed from many points. Here are four:

South terminus (Ashland): From the intersection of Oak and Nevada streets in the northern part of Ashland, go one block west on Nevada Street to Helman Street, and turn right on the narrow paved road that leads to the Ashland Dog Park. Parking is available. The trail begins just before you reach the parking area. For the first quarter mile or so, the trail runs next to the Ashland Wastewater Treatment Plant and then next to a stone yard. But it finally enters a riparian area, with large cottonwoods, some ponderosa pines, and wildflowers such as California poppies, storksbill, and a mint called purple deadnettle. At one point there is a small pond, that may have wood ducks, and green-winged teal.

Bear Creek Park in spring

Lynn Newbry Park (Talent): Use Exit 21 from I-5, and go toward Talent. The entrance to Lynn Newbry Park is less than 100 yards from the freeway, on the left. There are parking, playgrounds, and picnic tables, but no restrooms. The path toward the south (toward Ashland) is popular, and leads next to small marshes and a couple of small ponds. This section is excellent for woodland birds, such as robins, spotted towhees, song sparrows, and Bewick's wrens. In spring, the songs of the sparrows and the wrens are everywhere, although you may have to hunt a bit among the branches to spot the singers.

The larger of the two ponds near Lynn

Ring-necked Duck

Observation platform at Mingus Pond

Newbry Park usually has waterfowl. One worth looking for is the ring-necked duck, but don't waste your time looking for the ring on the neck. It is only visible at close range. A better mark is the conspicuous white ring around the bill, causing many people to wonder why it isn't called the "ring-*billed*" duck.

Bear Creek Park (Medford): This is essentially a city park. To get there, use Exit 27 from I-5, at Barnett Road. Go a short dis-tance east to a signal at Highland Drive, and turn left. There is an entrance to the park on the left, about 0.2 mile along Highland Drive. Another entrance can be reached by continuing on Highland Drive to Siskiyou Blvd., turning left, and going 0.1 mile to the entrance on the left. There are picnic tables, playgrounds, and a big skateboard park. The greenway trail next to the creek offers some natural surroundings.

North terminus (Central Point): To get to this terminus, use Exit 33 from I-5, and turn east on East Pine Street. Go 0.2 mile to Peninger Road (signal), and turn left. Then immediately turn right into the large dirt parking area. The trail goes to the right, under the bridge.

Roses at Jackson and Perkins Test Garden

Parts of the trail in this section run right next to the freeway, and there is a lot of industrial development on the opposite side of the creek. However, its saving grace is the existence of a delightful small pond, called **Mingus Pond,** about a half-mile along the trail. There is a neat little observation platform here that was constructed by the Boy Scouts, and you can sit at your leisure and watch the wildlife in the pond below. Lots of songbirds such as

Baby blue-eyes at Beekman Arboretum

song sparrows and yellow-rumped warblers love the heavy vegetation around the pond. There usually are waterfowl such as ring-decked ducks, mallards, and gadwalls. Once in a while you may be able to spot a green heron sitting quietly among the low branches next to the water.

Some other places in the Bear Creek Valley that are worth a visit are described in what follows. Lithia Park, in Ashland, is one of those places, but it has its own chapter.

There is for example, an area that some people call **Rosebud Lane.** To get there, use Exit 14 from I-5 (Highway 66), go east on Highway 66 about 5.0 miles to the Old Siskiyou Highway. There is a small amount of parking on the left, and an old paved road (blocked, but open to pedestrians) that leads to Emigrant Lake. The areas on both sides of this old road are crammed with rose bushes, and in June the area is almost solid rose blooms. This particular kind of rose, called dog rose, is an introduced species from Europe, but it is growing wild here. I don't mind that they aren't native. They are gorgeous.

For a different kind of rose experience, visit the **Jackson and Perkins** test rose garden. To get there, use Exit 27 from I-5, and turn west on Barnett Road. Go 0.4 mile to Riverside Avenue and turn left (south). The rose garden is next to the corporate offices of Jackson and Perkins, 1.1 miles south on Riverside Avenue. (Riverside Avenue is Highway 99, and on the way to Jackson and Perkins it changes its name to South Pacific Highway.) As you enter the driveway in front of the corporate offices, the experimental garden is on your right, and limited parking is available next to the garden.

Jacksonville is a delightful historical town. Jackson Creek, which runs through the town, is a tributary of Bear Creek. An especially nice natural experience is offered by the **Beekman Native Plant Arboretum.** The arboretum has a trail which is accessible to people with limited mobility. To get to the arboretum, turn east at the junction of California and

Gentner fritillaria

Fifth streets in Jacksonville, and go 0.2 mile on California Street to the Beekman House. The arboretum is directly behind the Beekman House.

There is a longer trail nearby (not for people with limited mobility), called the **Beekman Canyon Trail**, that makes a one mile loop up and over the nearby hill, beginning and ending at the arboretum. This trail leads through a forest of madrone, ponderosa, Douglas-fir, and, of course, poison oak.

The arboretum covers about three acres, and has native plants from eight habitat types, ranging from mixed forest to high desert. Many kinds of wildflowers can be found here and along the nearby Beekman Canyon Trail, depending upon the season. In April, baby blue-eyes lurk in the grass, and the woods nearby can be alive with shooting-stars and hound's tongue. Showy white trilliums are here and there, and, if you are especially fortunate, you may come upon a gorgeous tall lily called Gentner fritillaria.

Farther out in the valley, near Central Point, is the Agate Desert. This great, flat, sparsely-vegetated area with the unattractive name is where most of the industrial development in the Rogue Valley is located. But look again. The Nature Conservancy thought the botanical resources of this area were unusual, so they purchased an area at the northwest corner of Table Rock and Antelope Roads and named it the **Agate Desert Preserve.** In spring, this preserve is carpeted with wildflowers, such as goldfields and miniature lupine. It is worth a closer look. (Watch out for traffic on both Table Rock and Antelope Roads.)

Goldfields   **Miniature lupine**

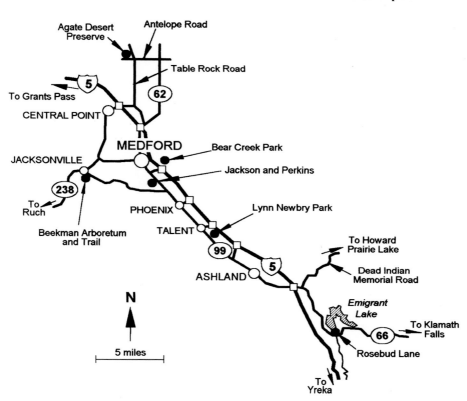

Agate Desert
Preserve

Antelope Road

Table Rock Road

5

To Grants Pass

CENTRAL POINT

62

MEDFORD

Bear Creek Park

JACKSONVILLE

Jackson and Perkins

238

To
Ruch

PHOENIX

Lynn Newbry Park

TALENT

Beekman Arboretum
and Trail

99

To Howard
Prairie Lake

Dead Indian
Memorial Road

5

ASHLAND

*Emigrant
Lake*

To Klamath
Falls

66

N

Rosebud Lane

5 miles

To
Yreka

Wood ducks (male and female) at Upper Duck Pond

11 Lithia Park

Ashland's gorgeous garden

I once was told that if I wanted to see wood ducks, I should go to Lithia Park's upper duck pond. This turned out to be good advice, although I later learned it works better in winter than in spring or summer. In spring and summer, the wood ducks are likely to be out somewhere on their breeding territories.

Lithia Park is more than just ducks, of course. It is a marvelous woodland park tucked into the edge of the City of Ashland, with a mountain stream, hiking trails, rhododendrons, azaleas, Japanese garden, playgrounds, and band shell. To some, it looks like a miniature version of the famous Golden Gate Park in San Francisco. And no wonder, because John McLaren, superintendent of Golden Gate Park, had a hand in the development of Lithia Park. Not all of McLaren's ideas were used. For example, he envisioned that the park

OPPOSITE PAGE: Walking path in Lithia Park

would include a mineral springs resort, with a sanitarium. This part of the plan did not take place. Instead, Lithia Park became a "passive park in a wilderness setting."

The park, in one form or another, has a 150-year history. Ashland got its start in 1852, and its starting place was where the Plaza now sits. Ashland Creek became the power source for a flour mill that stood for 50 years next door, at the entrance to today's park.

In 1893, the Chautauqua came to Ashland. The Chautauqua was a nationwide organization that was immensely popular at the time, and offered speakers on current events, concerts, classes, and roundtable discussions. A huge wooden building, large enough to accommodate 1000 people, was built by the Chautauqua Association on the hill above

Camellia

Rhododendron

Magnolia

Azalea

Ashland Creek, and the foundation of that building later was used for today's Elizabethan theater.

In the early Chautauqua days, people came by railroad and by wagon, and many of them set up their tents along the creek below the Chautauqua building. Gradually, a park came into being, owned by the Chautauqua Association, but open to the public. Proposals were made to create a city-owned park along the creek, and the people of Ashland, in 1908, voted to tax themselves for that purpose.

The old flour mill, which had fallen into disrepair and had become an eyesore, was removed. The grounds were landscaped, and paths were constructed. "Lithia Water," containing the mineral lithium, was piped in from springs east of the city, to an artificially constructed cave known as "Satan's Sulphur Grotto." There was even a free auto camp near where the park office is located today.

Today, the Chautauqua is gone, the "Sulphur Grotto" is gone, the auto camp is gone, and all that remains of the "Lithia Water" is a drinking fountain in the Plaza. But what we have is a beautiful park that has a half million visitors per year.

Lithia Park, as beautiful and tranquil as it may seem, has not always been so peaceful. At least twice, once in 1974 and again in 1996, devastating floods have swept down the creek and through the Plaza, destroying bridges and creating havoc. Each time, the citizens of Ashland have rallied to reconstruct their beloved park, and today it shows little evidence of the floods.

The park begins next to the Plaza in downtown Ashland. A trail guide can be purchased at the park office, which describes a one-mile route that will take you on a circuit completely around the park. The trail guide will help you

Japanese garden in spring

Japanese garden in autumn

Upper duck pond

identify the trees and shrubs you see, which are both native and introduced. Many of the trees, such as the magnolias, produce gorgeous blossoms in spring. The same is true of some of the abundant rhododendrons, camellias, and azaleas.

The **Japanese Garden** is a delight, especially in autumn, when it glows with color. The **Upper Duck Pond** is another special attraction, both for its landscaping, and for its resident ducks.

Ashland Creek runs the length of the park, and is the prototype of the perfect babbling mountain brook. American dippers are here, although most visitors overlook them. Each December, the Audubon Society conducts a "dipper walk" along the creek, usually turning up 5 to 7 dippers.

OPPOSITE PAGE:
Autumn in Lithia Park

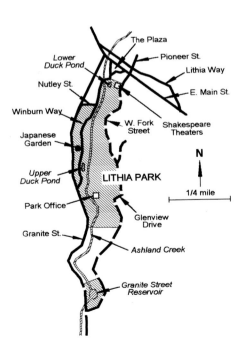

The Siskiyou crest near Dutchman Peak

12 The Siskiyou Crest

Mount Ashland to Dutchman Peak

In July, many residents of the warm Rogue Valley may not realize that they live within a short distance of a cool subalpine paradise.   True, they can look up and see Mount Ashland, with a few streaks of snow persisting into summer, but the mountain seems like a familiar and ordinary fixture, with its ski runs and its radar dome on top, giving little hint of what lies beyond.

But beyond the mountain, on what the U.S. Forest Service calls **"The Siskiyou Loop,"** the road runs for 13 miles at the 6000 to 7000-foot level, often rising into wonderful green meadows bordered by clumps of fir, and strewn with wildflowers.

The full route, from I-5 to Jacksonville, is 55 miles, and you have to be prepared for 23 miles of dusty road if you're going to take this trip. However, even on busy weekends there

OPPOSITE PAGE: Mount Shasta from near Mount Ashland

generally are not many cars, and during the week you may not encounter any other cars at all. Early July is the time to go. Earlier than that, and the road is closed by snow. Later than that, and the wildflowers have faded. It can be an all-day trip, so take lunch and drinking water.

The departure point is Exit 6 from I-5, south of Ashland, where the sign says, "Mount Ashland." Go 0.9 mile on the frontage road, and turn west on Mount Ashland Road. Mileages are reckoned from that point. At these relatively low elevations, there are chicory and bachelor's buttons, both of them introduced plants.

As you progress toward Mount Ashland, the forest gets better and better. Paintbrush and a lavender-pink penstemon line the road edges. There is a large parking area at 6.9

Western blue flax

Pussypaws

Paintbrush

Green-tailed towhee

miles, where **Bull Gap Road** comes in. It is surrounded by a forest of Douglas-fir and white fir, with wildflowers tucked among the trees. When I was there last, there were at least two hermit thrushes singing, right in the middle of the day. The song of the hermit thrush has often been described as the most beautiful of all bird songs, but it is usually heard at dusk, instead of in midday.

Spreading phlox on Dutchman Peak

The parking lot for the Mount Ashland ski area comes at 8.7 miles, and the pavement ends at 9.1 miles. The next 13 miles are narrow and often one-way, but negotiable by an ordinary car in good weather. The Forest Service designates it as Road 20. Along the way, there are some sensational views of Mount Shasta toward the south.

In July, wildflowers are profuse along the slopes next to the road. Scarlet gilia, woolly sunflower, and sulphur flower are common. Almost hidden in the foliage are the tiny mariposa tulips called "pussy ears."

At 10.2 miles, the road to the top of **Mount Ashland** branches off. It is 1.2 miles to the top of the mountain, along a rough one-way road that probably is not everyone's cup of tea. A high-clearance vehicle is desirable. The top of the mountain itself is not especially beautiful, with roads here and there, tall antennas, a radar dome, and a ski lift. But the view is

Davidson penstemon on Mount Ashland

sensational, with Mount McLaughlin to the north, and Mount Shasta to the south. Mount Ashland, at 7,533 feet, is the highest peak in the Siskiyous, and in fact is the highest peak in Oregon west of the Cascades. Dutchman Peak, a few miles further on, is almost as high, at 7,418 feet.

On the way up the rough road, fox sparrows and green-tailed towhees sing from the bushes and from the scattered trees, sounding so much alike that you can't be sure which is which. In early July, patches of spreading phlox are scattered here and there, as well as western blue flax. On top of the mountain, a rock wren was singing when I was there the last time, and a prairie falcon was darting about. A special payoff was the mats of rose-purple Davidson penstemon, located virtually on top of the mountain.

Back down on Road 20, the wonderful meadows of **Grouse Gap** soon come into view, and the road to the Grouse Gap Shelter (restrooms) is encountered at 11.1 miles, measuring from I-5. Grouse Gap Shelter is an attractive structure, presumably built for the convenience of hikers on the Pacific Coast Trail (PCT), but I've never seen anyone camping there. However, it is frequently used by picnickers, and people often leave their cars near the shelter while they day-hike on the PCT. The road edges are covered with mats of tiny dwarf lupine.

From Grouse Gap, the road continues west, sometimes on one side of the crest and sometimes on the other, but remaining mostly between 6000 and 7000 feet. At 15.9 miles, a high-standard gravel road (Road 22) comes in from the right. This road goes to **Wagner Gap** and then to Talent, in about 17 miles. Approximately 2.8 miles down this road is a wet meadowy slope covered with tiger lilies, corn lily, lupine, cow parsnip, and bog-orchid.

The lowest point on the crest road (5900 feet) is at **Siskiyou Gap**, at 16.6 miles. Siskiyou Gap is noteworthy from a geological point of view, because it represents the contact zone between serpentine rocks to the west, and granitic rocks to the east. From Siskiyou Gap back

Beargrass

to I-5, including Mount Ashland, the rocks are basically granitic in nature, somewhat unusual for Oregon's landscape, which is mostly dominated by volcanic rocks.

For the next 5 miles or so beyond Siskiyou Gap, the forest becomes rather dry, but the dryness is compensated for by extensive clumps of beargrass, with their two-foot high white plumes shining in the forest. Then, at 21.3 miles, you come into the open once more, with marvelous sweeping views up to the subalpine country around Dutchman Peak.

This is wildflower country. The dominant flower is balsamroot, with clumps covered with silvery-gray leaves and brilliant yellow sunflower-type flowers. Almost as dominant is the scarlet gilia, which some people call "skyrocket." Along with these are red columbine, and yellow sedum, sometimes called stonecrop. In many dry, sunny places, the surface is covered with ground-hugging pussypaws, making a pink mat.

Jackson Gap (22.2 miles from I-5) at 7,061 feet is the high point of the main loop road. From here, a rough road leads 2 miles to the top of **Dutchman Peak,** where there is a lookout. From the gap, Road 20 goes downhill above the lush green bowl of Silver Fork Basin, and leads ultimately to Ruch and Jacksonville. For the next mile and a half, the slopes below Dutchman Peak are watered by springs, and have a profusion of wildflowers, including almost every variety seen previously along the road, such as scarlet gilia, paintbrush, penstemon, and western blue flax.

At 24.4 miles there is a major cross-roads, with roads leading in six directions. Fortunately, the correct road to Jacksonville is labeled Road 20. It now becomes a high-standard gravel road, changes to pavement at 32.7 miles, and reaches Jacksonville at 55.0 miles.

Scarlet gilia

At Daffodil Hill

13 Upper Rogue

And on, to Huckleberry Mountain Meadow

Most people think of Highway OR 62 as the road to Crater Lake, and so it is. But it is also a road to some special places of beauty all its own, including waterfalls and mountain meadows. From Medford, it is 19.4 miles to where the highway crosses the Rogue River at Shady Cove. From then on, the highway is never very far from the river.

Before leaving Shady Cove, it is worthwhile to visit **Daffodil Hill.** The visit should be made in early March, because this is when the daffodils are in full bloom. If you are going north on OR 62, you must turn left on Rogue River Road, just as you cross over the bridge and enter Shady Cove. It is 0.3 mile on Rogue River Road to Sawyer Road, where you turn right. In March, there will be signs posted, directing you to Daffodil Hill.

OPPOSITE PAGE: Rabbit Ears

81

Boardwalk at McGregor Park

The daffodils begin a short distance up Sawyer Road, and extend for a mile or so on both sides of the road, among the pines and oaks. The plantings are maintained by the residents, and are extensive. More than anything, they resemble splashes of yellow sunshine among the trees.

About 9 miles north of Shady Cove on OR 62, just beyond Casey State Park, Takelma Drive goes to the left, and leads to McGregor Park and to the "Holy Water." **McGregor Park** is just 0.3 mile up Takelma Drive. It is a delightful spot, and was constructed by the Corps Of Engineers when they built the big dam that holds back Lost Creek Lake. There are green lawns, picnic tables, restrooms, and a system of paved short trails that lead through the woods and along the river.

To get to the **"Holy Water,"** continue on Takelma Drive for 0.2 mile past McGregor Park, and turn right. Go past the parking lot next to the small dam at the fish hatchery, and turn left on a partly paved narrow road that comes just before the fish hatchery dam. This road has turnouts and park benches, and extends upstream about 0.5 mile along the river.

This part of the Rogue River, between the big dam upstream and the smaller dam at the fish hatchery, is a quiet section that is attractive both to ducks and to fly fishermen. Its name of "Holy Water" was given many years ago because of the huge trout that gathered below the Lost Creek Lake dam after its completion in 1977.

The Holy Water is open to fishing year-round, but only for

Barrow's Goldeneyes at "Holy Water"

fly-fishing, and for "catch-and-release." The official name of this section is **Rivers Edge Park,** and there is another section of Rivers Edge Park on the opposite bank. In the wintertime, you can sit inside your car and watch the hundreds of ducks that gather on the Holy Water at that time of year, including the especially beautiful ones such as common goldeneye, Barrow's goldeneye, bufflehead, and hooded merganser. If you are so inclined, you can visit the nearby fish hatchery.

Back on OR 62, you soon come to the large bridge across Lost Creek Reservoir, called Petyon Bridge. At the north end of the bridge is Lewis Road (on the left), and about 100 yards down Lewis Road is one of the trailheads for the **Rogue River Trail.** The trail itself extends for many miles along the Rogue River, but even if you take only a short walk along the trail, heading upstream, you can encounter a large number of wildflowers, including iris, blue dicks, silver lupine, and an astonishing number of pussy ears if you happen to be there at the right time.

The turnoff for **Mill Creek Falls** is about 21 miles north of Shady Cove, on OR 62. From the turnoff, it is 0.9 mile to the parking area, following signs. From the parking area a good trail leads to Mill Creek Falls, a distance of about 0.3 mile. There is another fall, called **Barr Creek Falls,** just 0.1 mile further. There are good viewpoints for both, but neither viewpoint is protected by a fenced barrier, making them risky for children. The trail has Pacific dogwood, western trillium, vanilla leaf, and western starflower.

The falls are highly scenic, and drop directly into the Rogue River. Mill Creek Falls in 173 feet high. Barr Creek Falls is slightly higher, and is listed as 175 to 200 feet high. To my eye, Barr Creek Falls is the more attractive of the two, although Mill Creek Falls gets most of the publicity.

Barr Creek Falls

Western starflower

Vine maple in autumn

Continuing up OR 62, you enter heavy forest near the Prospect Ranger Station, about 42 miles from Medford. Most of the highway above Shady Cove has great beauty, but when you enter the forest near the Prospect Ranger Station, it is like entering a different world. The trees lining the road recall sections of the Redwood Highway.

In spring, the forest glows with the white flowers of the Pacific dogwood. In October, the leaves of the dogwood turn a delicate rosy color. Also, in fall, the vine maples turn red in the sun and yellow in the shade. As you drive through the thick forest, the leaves appear to have an internal glow, lighting up the woods.

The U.S. Forest Service map shows a "point of interest" along this section of the road called "Mammoth Pines." Unfortunately, the largest pine, that was the centerpiece of this attraction, died a few years ago, shortly after the Forest Service map went to print. Consequently, the site has been closed, although the old asphalt loop road and parking lot are still there, slowly decaying.

Beginning at Natural Bridge, there are several special attractions, and three unusually nice campgrounds, that come in the four-mile stretch between Natural Bridge and the intersection of OR 62 and OR 230.

The turnoff for **Natural Bridge** and **Natural Bridge Campground** is about 52 miles from Medford. There is a large parking lot, restrooms, and a paved barrier-free trail about 0.3 mile that leads to the river and along it.

Vanilla leaf

Several viewing platforms give vantage points to see the river as it enters an old lava tube and then surges forth again downstream, creating the natural "bridge." The geological phenomenon of the bridge is interesting enough, but the trail has a natural beauty that is an attraction in itself. The nearby campground is delightful, with many nicely placed sites along the river and paved interior roads. However, it seems to be the case that the sites are almost always fully occupied.

The next point of interest is **Union Creek Campground**, the adjacent Union Creek Resort, and Beckie's Cafe, all of which are about one mile from Natural Bridge. The Union Creek Campground is a big one, with many attractive sites along Union Creek, and paved interior roads. In October, when the campground is practically empty of people, this may be the best place of all for autumn color.

The vine maples and dogwoods are everywhere throughout the campground, especially along Union Creek itself and along the Rogue River. The **Rogue River Trail** runs along the

river's edge near the campground, and provides access to some of the best sites for fall color. The trail can be accessed from the lower parts of the campground.

Near the Union Creek Campground is Beckie's, a small cafe that has been a landmark from the time tourists starting coming through. When my wife and I first started going to Beckie's, we wondered which one of the women who seemed to be in charge was the one called "Beckie." Then we learned how totally off base we were. In the first place, since the cafe has been there since the 1920s, "Beckie" would have to be over 100 years old. Also, "Beckie" doesn't refer to a woman at all. It is the nickname of Ed Beckelhymer, who built a garage and delicatessen there in 1921.

Just beyond Union Creek is **Rogue Gorge Viewpoint,** a popular site that might be

AT RIGHT: Rogue Gorge

considered the centerpiece of the Upper Rogue. There is parking, a restroom building, and a delightful paved trail about ¼ mile long, barrier-free, that leads along the edge of the gorge. There are observation platforms, and one of them literally overhangs the lip of the gorge. At this point, the gorge is deeper (45 feet) than it is wide (25 feet from the edge of the platform to the opposite rim).

Below, the water surges in a white torrent between the narrow walls. It is said that the gorge was created by the collapse of an old lava tube, and there are actually a couple of collapsed tubes visible on the opposite side.

About a mile beyond Union Creek is **Farewell Bend Campground,** another delightful campground with many riverside sites, but also a place where the sites seem almost always to be occupied -- at least the nicest ones.

The junction between OR 62 and OR 230 comes about a mile beyond Farewell Bend. At this point, OR 62 swings east toward Crater Lake, and the Rogue River route continues on OR 230.

Much of this section of OR 230 is reminiscent of the beautiful forest corridor near Prospect, described above. Several times, the road comes close to the river, which here flows smoothly through grassy banks and lush forest. About 5 miles beyond the junction where OR 62 turns off to Crater Lake, there are views of **Rabbit Ears,** a remarkable remnant of an old volcano. **Highway Falls** (a broad waterfall 5 to 10 feet high, visible from the highway) is about 7.3 miles beyond the Crater Lake junction. For about the next 1.5 miles the highway runs close to the river, offering attractive views.

The turnoff to **National Creek Falls** is 5.9 miles north of the junction of OR 62 and OR 230. Turn on Forest Road 6530 (paved), and follow signs for 3.5 miles to the parking area. The falls are attractive, and about 50 to 70 feet high. The trail is about 0.5 mile long, well constructed, and descends in a series of switchbacks, for an elevation loss (and subsequent regaining) of about 200 feet. In spring, the trail will have many wildflowers, including bunchberry dogwood, vanilla leaf, kinnikinnick and yellow-leaved iris. There may be mosquitoes.

Excursion to Huckleberry Mountain Meadow. The region around Union Creek and Rogue

AT LEFT:
National Creek Falls

AT RIGHT:
Highway Falls

Gorge lies at an elevation of about 3400 feet, but Huckleberry Mountain Meadow is more than 2000 feet higher, which means that it is cool in the summer, but also means that the road is closed by snow and fallen trees until about July.

The meadow is lovely, and is full of corn lilies and crowded with wildflowers in early summer. There is a nice campground, called **Huckleberry Mountain Campground,** that has never had anyone camping in it when we've been there, but is reportedly used more heavily in late summer when the huckleberries get ripe. The campsites are well separated, and are located along a loop road that surrounds the meadow.

The huckleberry bushes indeed are there, extending everywhere under the trees around the meadow. If the huckleberry-pickers are there, then that means the bears might be there too, because bears like huckleberries just as much as people do.

Western prince's pine

Here's how to get there. From Union Creek, continue north on OR 62, and follow it east toward Crater Lake, from the point where OR 230 joins OR 62. Go 5.7 miles on OR 62 to a

point just beyond the Thousand Springs Sno-Park, where Forest Road 60 comes in. Along this stretch of OR 62, wildflowers hide in the forest. A flower well worth looking for is the tiny western prince's pine, which may be completely overlooked if you don't search for it.

At the Thousand Springs Sno-Park, turn right. It is 4.0 miles to Huckleberry Mountain Campground, on a gravel road that is narrow in places. The first part of the road travels through lodgepole pine forest -- the kind in which all the trees are small, about the same size, and crowded together. Then the forest gets better. Side roads take off in a couple of places, but the thing to do is to stick to Forest Road 60.

About a mile from the campground, you begin to enter nice meadows, with great wildflowers in mid-July, such as wandering daisies, paintbrush, red columbine, mountain owlclover, and scarlet gilia. The meadow next to the campground, the one I have called "Huckleberry Mountain Meadow," is apparently called "Crawford Creek Meadow" by the U.S. Forest Service, although the name does not appear on the maps for the area. But Crawford Creek drains the area, so it is apparently the source of the name.

Under the bushes around the meadow, in the shade, are Columbia windflowers, and a tiny blue trumpet-shaped flower that hides in the grass. This little flower bears the delightful name of Mt. Mazama mountaintrumpet, and is a plant that is special to the southern Cascades around Crater Lake and Mount McLaughlin.

An optional route for the return is to continue on through Huckleberry Mountain Campground on Forest Road 60, which will bring you back to OR 62 in 11 miles or so, about 4 miles south of Union Creek. The road becomes paved (although the pavement is deteriorating) after 4 miles, and is one-way in most sections, with turnouts.

AT LEFT:
Wandering daisies at Huckleberry Mountain Meadow

Mountain owl-clover

Yellow-leaved iris

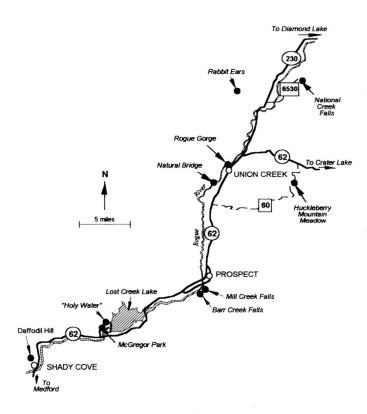

Butte Falls

14 Butte Falls and Whiskey Springs
And to the edge of Sky Lakes Wilderness

Butte Falls is the prototype of the Oregon logging town. Around 1900, a mill was constructed next to the nearby falls, and by 1910 there was a railroad between Butte Falls and Medford. The railroad continued in operation until 1960, when the coming of log trucks made it obsolete.

The old mill by the falls on Big Butte Creek is gone, but the falls are there. It is a delightful spot for a visit, especially in early summer when the wildflowers are blooming. If you include the excursion to Blue Rock, it is an all-day trip, so take your lunch and some drinking water.

To get to Butte Falls, from the junction of I-5 and OR 62 in Medford (Exit 30), go north on OR 62 for 14.0 miles to Butte Falls Road and turn right. At 15.4 miles, you enter the

---

OPPOSITE PAGE: Chicory

Common wintergreen

White bog-orchid

edge of town. Falls Road is on the left, and the sign says **"Big Butte Creek Falls. Historic mill site. 0.6 mi."** The road is mostly one-way and is gravel, but is okay for ordinary passenger cars. It leads past the Butte Falls Recycling Depot, and down the hill to a large parking area next to the falls, with a short path leading to an observation platform.

The falls are not high, perhaps eight feet or so, but the ledge that produces the falls extends across the entire creek, so the total effect is impressive. Near the viewing platform are some concrete foundations belonging to the old mill.

In mid-July, the roadsides and parking area can be alive with wildflowers. Blue chicory and multicolored sweet peas are the most visible, and both of them are transplants from Europe. It is interesting to note that chicory has taken over most of the continent. It favors roadsides and open fields, and its cheerful blue flowers can be seen in almost every state. Chicory might even be considered the national wildflower, if it was a native plant.

There are even a few tall red-pink fireweed plants along the road, and blackberry bushes of two kinds are next to the parking lot. One is the familiar Himalayan blackberry, which seems to be everywhere in western Oregon, and produces abundant berries that are picked enthusiastically. The other is the evergreen, or "cutleaf" blackberry, which is not so widespread, and possesses interesting deeply cleft leaves. Both are imports from Europe that have escaped from cultivation.

When we were there, in mid-July, a hermit thrush was singing its beautiful song in the woods, and an osprey flew down the stream, carrying a fish. Somewhere, out of sight on the creek, the rattling sound of a belted kingfisher could be heard. Red-breasted sapsuckers can be seen. Sapsuckers really do suck the sap of trees, and bore multiple holes in the bark to stimulate the flow of sap.

Back on the main Butte Falls Road, directly across from the road to the falls, is **Fairy Glen Botanical Park.** The trail lies on the old railroad grade, so it is easy walking. Besides lots of chicory, sweet peas, and Himalayan blackberries, there are bachelor's buttons, white yarrow, mule's ears, and tiny white daisies (dog fennel). In July, we heard a Cassin's vireo singing, an acorn woodpecker making its raucous *ya-cob ya-cob* sound, and saw a brilliant orange male Bullock's oriole darting about.

In the center of the town of Butte Falls there is a crossroads and a flashing red traffic signal. This crossroads will be used as a reference point (0.0 miles) for what follows.

Leaving town, and proceeding to the east, the **Butte Falls Fish Hatchery** comes at 0.9 mile. There is an attractive shaded picnic site just inside the gate. Restrooms are located near the visitor parking, about 200 yards further on. The hatchery raises salmon and rainbow trout.

After you leave the hatchery, the road to Prospect comes after only 0.1 mile. If you plan to take the excursion to Blue Rock (described later), this is the best road to take. Just across the bridge, and on the left, there is a picnic area, with sites situated along the creek.

Proceeding to the east on Butte Falls Road (County Road 821), you come in 9.4 miles to the turnoff for Whiskey Springs Campground. Along the way, the main access road to **Willow Lake Recreation Area** is at 7.6 miles. Willow Lake includes a campground, picnic area, and boat-launching facilities. There is another road a mile further on, which leads to the east shore of the lake.

Fireweed

Red-breasted sapsucker

Mount McLoughlin from Blue Rock

The road ahead provides some great views of Mount McLoughlin, and wildflowers such as scarlet gilia, blue penstemon, and lupine become more frequent. There are even wild strawberries lurking inconspicuously on the ground among the pine trees. Each berry is only the size of a small pea.

After turning off on the road for Whiskey Springs, the paved road ends at 0.3 mile, at the campground and day-use area. The **Whiskey Springs Nature Trail** begins at the day-use area, and makes a round trip of about 1 mile, going all the way around an old beaver pond. The trail is wheelchair accessible, and has several benches for resting.

The forest is mostly Douglas-fir, grand fir, incense cedar, dogwood, and hazelnut. In two places, boardwalks cross over the small stream, and plants such as tiger lily, white bog-orchid, and yellow mimulus grow in such wet places. In the drier locations there are wild roses, giant lupine, common wintergreen, Oregon geranium, Oregon grape, ocean spray, and spiraea. The campground is spacious and well developed, with paved roads. The U.S. Forest Service rates it as a "high-usage" campground.

Excursion to Blue Rock. Blue Rock is a high point (6560+ feet elevation), right on the border of the Sky Lakes Wilderness Area. At one time, there was a Forest Service lookout there, but now there are only old concrete foundations. It is a commanding high point, with sensational views of Mt. McLoughlin. The downside is that the last half-mile of road is extremely rocky and rough. It's the sort of road where you take your car at your own risk.

Even high-clearance vehicles run the risk of tire damage. I once had two flat tires at the same time on just such a road, caused by sharp rocks, and had to be hauled out. You might want to walk this stretch of road, instead of taking your car.

If you want to go to Blue Rock, here's how to get there. From near the fish hatchery, 1.0 mile from Butte Falls, take the high-standard road to Prospect. It is 8.7 miles to Lodgepole Road, on the right. This is another high-standard, paved road, that becomes Forest Road 34, and joins Forest Road 37 in 8.3 miles. Most of it is two-way, but the last 1.5 miles is one-way (paved), with turnouts. The South Fork Campground is located 7.7 miles from where you turned on Lodgepole Road. It is a nice little campground, but dusty.

Oregon geranium

After joining Forest Road 37, go south 9.2 miles to Forest Road 3770, on the left, which is the road that will take you to Blue Rock. About 7 miles of Road 37 is paved, one-way, with turnouts. After that, it becomes a good gravel road. Road 3770 is also a good gravel road until the last mile or so. The first part of this last mile requires caution because the road has rather abrupt drainage ditches cut across it, which can cause unpleasant surprises if you're going very fast. The last half of it is the rough, rocky road I mentioned earlier.

It is 6.4 miles on Road 3770 to the end, through lovely forest. When we were there in mid-July, the roadsides were literally lined with scarlet gilia, coyote mint, and lupine. At 5.4 miles there is a lovely little meadow, with a trailhead for the Sky Lakes Wilderness.

If you make it to the top, the view of Mt. McLoughlin is outstanding, and so are the wildflowers. Early in the season, there is spreading phlox everywhere. A little later, and the scarlet gilias take over. Tiny ground rose bushes are scattered

Sulphur flower

Coyote mint

among the rocks, some only a few inches in height. Red columbine, sulphur flower, and coyote mint fill in the spaces. As a final bonus, when we were there, a hermit thrush could be heard singing in the forest.

Little ground rose on Blue Rock

OPPOSITE PAGE:
   Willow Lake and
      Mount McLoughlin

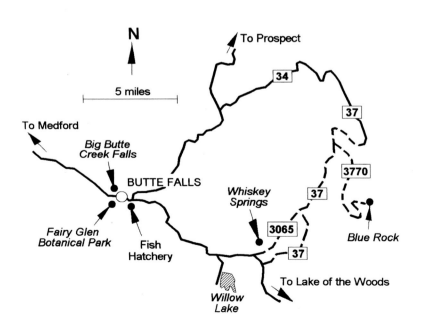

Pacific dogwood leaves in autumn

15 Fish Lake Trail

Plus Forest Road 37

    If you were to set up some criteria for a perfect walk, then you might include the following conditions: There should be (1) a beautiful forest; (2) a gorgeous creek; (3) an almost level trail, with little climbing; (4) and it should be easy to get to. These criteria are all fulfilled, with something left over for good measure, by the **Fish Lake Trail,** where it runs next to the North Fork of Little Butte Creek, below Fish Lake.

    Here's how to get there. From Medford, go 28 miles east on OR 140 to Forest Road 37, on the right. From Klamath Falls go 39 miles west on OR 140 (7.8 miles beyond the Lake of the Woods turnoff). The parking area for the trail is 0.5 mile south on Forest Road 37, directly across from the North Fork Campground. Bicycles are permitted on the trail, but not horses. A Northwest Forest Parking Pass is required. (These can be purchased at ranger stations.)

OPPOSITE PAGE: North Fork Little Butte Creek

Oak leaves in autumn

From the parking area it is only 0.6 mile to the dam that holds back Fish Lake. The trail is almost always within view of the creek, which alternates between rapids and long stretches of quiet water, bordered by meadowlike grassy marshes. From time to time, old stumps of trees can be spotted near the creek that have been gnawed by beavers. There are even the remains of an old beaver dam, but I have not been able to see any recent beaver sign.

The forest appears almost primeval, with huge Douglas-firs, grand firs, and western white pines. In sunny places, where the trail is covered with fallen fir needles, a wonderful balsam-like odor fills the air. Occasionally, old stumps can be spotted, raising the question as to why just a few large trees were cut, apparently far in the past, and why so many trees were left untouched.

On one visit in early fall, the leaves of some of the oaks were showing a fiery red color. Normally, in fall, they are golden brown. The leaves on the Pacific dogwood trees were turning rose-red. In place of the marvelous white dogwood flowers of spring, there now were tight red berry clumps. The related creek dogwoods were showing small, waxy green berries. Huckleberry bushes were scattered below the trees, but people had been there before us and had cleaned the bushes of most of their berries.

Here and there among the giant trees were small, scruffy-looking Pacific yew trees, their leaf-fronds looking like those of coast redwoods, and their bright

Berrylike aril of Pacific yew

red fruits looking disturbingly like red huckleberries. (These flesh-covered seeds are called "arils.") Since the yew seeds are **poisonous,** this reminded us that many of the fruits of the forest can be unwholesome, or even deadly.

Not many years ago, the bark of yew trees was harvested to a limited degree, because it could be made into a cancer-fighting agent. Then, when it was discovered that the same agent could be synthesized in the lab, the harvesting was discontinued.

Knowing that many berries are either inedible or poisonous, we have generally contented ourselves with picking the blue huckleberries, and, at lower elevations, the wonderful blackberries. And, if were are fortunate enough to find any, we love the tiny wild strawberries, which hide themselves so well among the leaves.

In spring, the brilliant white flowers of the dogwood trees clamor for attention. The forest floor along the trail is carpeted with greenery, with the lovely white blossoms of the Columbia windflowers seeming to mirror the dogwood blooms.

Tiny wild rose bushes line the trail in places. The lovely pink flowers of spring are no longer present in September, and the places of the flowers are taken by miniature red rose hips.

At the right time of year, in June, the bright orange flowers of the western trumpet honeysuckle might be discovered. Hidden in the greenery of the forest floor are tiny plants such as queen's cup, common wintergreen, and Pacific starflower. On one occasion, I discovered a strange little orchid, called spotted coralroot, right beside the trail.

Occasionally, cliffs of blocky lava are visible through the forest on the opposite side of the creek, representing a portion of the huge lava fields that cover the slopes of

Pacific dogwood

Western trumpet honeysuckle

Queen's cup

nearby Brown Mountain. The lava serves to remind us of the massive volcanic forces that shaped the Cascade range.

Lots of birds and other wildlife inhabit this spot. American dippers (still called *water ouzels* by some people, including me) can usually be spotted on rocks in the stream, doing their constant bobbing movements that give them their name of "dipper."

Red-breasted nuthatches can almost always be heard giving their *ank! ank! ank!* in the forest, and belted kingfishers call out their loud rattle as they fly along the stream. Even great blue herons and great egrets sometimes are spotted in the marshy areas. Chipmunks and golden-mantled ground squirrels are common.

The dam, when reached, appears intrusive. Yet, according to my *Atlas of Oregon Lakes,* if the dam were not there, then Fish Lake would be much smaller than it is, and the lovely North Fork would also be much smaller, because the natural inflow to the lake is not significant, according to the *Atlas.* In 1915, the Bureau of Reclamation constructed the rock fill dam. Then, in 1923 a canal and tunnel were constructed from Fourmile Lake, on the other side of the Cascade divide, to send water into Fish Lake and thus into the North Fork. (See Chapter 18, on Lake of the Woods.)

As a result of the above, much of the water we see in the beautiful North Fork actually comes from the Klamath Basin. It is heavily managed water, and its ultimate destiny is to go into the system of the Medford Irrigation District. As

American dipper

far as this serene spot is concerned, it doesn't seem to matter, and we can still enjoy its beauty.

Fish Lake itself is a lovely lake, generally giving little hint that it has a dam at the lower end. (At least it doesn't until late summer, when draw-down marks begin to show around the lake.) There are access roads from OR 140, 2 miles east of Forest Road 37.

Forest Road 37 is a delight. In fact, the part of the road near the Fish Lake Trail is one of the better places for dogwood-viewing. It is a high-standard paved road that extends for 8 miles from OR 140 to Dead Indian Memorial Road. For most of that distance, the route lies through fine, beautiful forest. In late summer, the roadsides are lined with fireweed, common mullein, chicory, and pearly everlasting.

Spotted coralroot

Mountain bluebird

16 Mountain Prairies
Lakes, forests, mountains, and meadows

In Colorado, the vast mountain meadows are called "parks." In our part of the west they are often called "prairies," and Southern Oregon abounds with them: Wood River Valley, Klamath Marsh, Langell Valley, and Poe Valley, among others. One of the best -- Howard Prairie -- is perched at an elevation of almost 5000 feet in the mountains above Ashland. This is mountain bluebird country.

From Exit 14 on I-5 in Ashland, go 0.6 mile east on OR 66 to Dead Indian Memorial Road, and turn left. Dead Indian Memorial Road ascends the mountain in sweeping curves, first passing through grassy slopes studded with oaks, and then into mature pine-fir forest. In spring, the grassy slopes are covered in places with magnificent patches of purple-pink vetch. Of the ten species of vetch known to be in Oregon, seven are not native, including this one, winter vetch. But the purple-pink hillsides are so gorgeous that it doesn't seem to matter.

OPPOSITE PAGE: Howard Prairie and Mount McLaughlin

Winter vetch along Dead Indian Memorial Road

About 13 miles up Dead Indian Memorial Road, the road passes over the crest, in a beautiful mixed forest of true fir and Douglas-fir. Howard Prairie lies about three miles beyond. However, it is worthwhile to take a detour on Shale City Road, by turning left about 6.6 miles from OR 66. Shale City Road makes a ten-mile loop, partly paved, and returns to Dead Indian Memorial Road just on the east side of the crest.

Shale City Road is also the access to the **Grizzly Peak Trail,** which is a popular day hike. The turnoff, a good gravel road, that leads to the Grizzly Peak trail is 2.9 miles on Shale City Road from Dead Indian Memorial Road, on the left. In 0.8 mile you come to a saddle where a transmission line goes through. At the saddle, take the road to the left that says "Trail." It is 0.8 mile (mostly one-way) further to the trailhead, with parking for several cars.

The trail leads through beautiful forest. The distance to the viewpoint overlooking Ashland is about two miles one-way (moderately easy). In spring, Columbia windflower and western trillium are everywhere, and the delicate flowers of woodland star show up here and there. The leaves of wild ginger conceal strange-looking flowers, and the spikes of striped coralroot occasionally show up. In July there are masses of tower delphinium, and by late August the forest seems full of the red berries of baneberry.

The first mile is spent in climbing onto the ridge of the mountain, and the second mile follows the undulating ridge to the viewpoint at the end. On the ridgetop, the forest begins to open up into green meadows, with lupine and blue stickseed. Toward the end of the ridge, the forest was burned by the East Antelope Fire of 2002, and for a period of time a temporary trail was provided to avoid the burned area.

The trail passes close to the true summit of Grizzly Peak (5920 feet). However, the summit doesn't offer good views, so the trail continues on to the point marked "Grizzly, 5747 feet" on the topographic map. From here, there are great views of Ashland, and this is the point that people generally label as "Grizzly Peak" when it is seen from below. The rocky soil supports wildflowers such as Siskiyou onion, yellow salsify, bluehead gilia, and sulphur flower.

Royal Jacob's ladder

Wild ginger

Western trillium

Woodland star

Satyr anglewing butterfly

After you return to your car and come back down to Shale City Road, if you turn to the right this brings you back to Dead Indian Memorial Road. If you turn to the left instead, you will come back to Dead Indian Memorial Road in 6.9 miles. This part of Shale City Road is mostly gravel, but it is well-graded. There will be a road intersecting Shale City Road in 0.1 mile, and you should go left at this point, but at every other intersection, keep right.

Shale City Road makes a loop around the mountain, passing through a fine forest and near delightful meadows that lie on or near the top of the ridge. Great views of Mount McLoughlin lie to the northeast, and Mount Ashland, in the opposite direction, is even visible at one point.

In June, after the snow is gone, the roadsides and meadows abound with wildflowers, including western trillium (in both white and purple colors), Henderson fawn lily, larkspur, tiny blue-eyed Mary, pussy ears, and shooting stars. In the meadows you will find small inconspicuous flowers such as dwarf waterleaf and dwarf hesperochiron. On one of our trips, in late May, a neat discovery was a satyr anglewing butterfly.

AT RIGHT:
Striped coralroot

By July other wildflowers appear, such as Oregon geranium, Washington lily, and masses of paintbrush.

After you return to Dead Indian Memorial Road and head east, the great meadows of **Howard Prairie** soon come into view, with Mount McLoughlin looming in the background. In spring, when Mount McLoughlin is decorated with snow fields, and the meadows are green, I don't think I know of a more sensational view. In June, portions of the prairie turn a bluish color with common camas. Most of the mountain prairies in this region get varying amounts of camas in spring, and in some instances the camas can be so dense that parts of the meadows may appear more blue than green.

An interesting question that arises here is: just where, exactly, is the Cascade crest? It turns out that this question has a surprisingly complex answer. Before humans began altering the flow of water courses, the high point over which Dead Indian Memorial Road passes was *not* the Cascade crest. Today, it is. What happened?

As you are heading east, the stream that runs parallel to Dead Indian Memorial Road on your right is Dead Indian Creek. Left to its own devices, the creek would intersect the road just about where the flattest part of Howard Prairie begins, would run under the road, and then down to the north, eventually to empty into the Rogue River. Thus, under those circumstances, the crest would lie along the ridge to the south of Dead Indian Creek.

But, just where the stream meets the road, there is a diversion dam that interrupts its historical flow, and instead sends the water from Dead Indian Creek through a ditch into **Howard Prairie Lake.** Howard Prairie Lake drains into the Klamath River, so the flow from Dead Indian Creek now belongs to the Klamath drainage,

Common camas

Sandhill crane

instead of to the Rogue. As a consequence of this diversion, the crest is now the high point you came over on Dead Indian Memorial Road.

After you pass the diversion dam, and are on the more or less flat surface of Howard Prairie, you actually cross a point where the water on one side of you would flow to the east, and on the other side, to the west. Thus, at this one point at least, Howard Prairie itself is the Cascade crest, a most un-crestlike state of affairs.

But wait. Howard Prairie Lake is a reservoir, and has a dam. Most of the water coming from the lake, instead of flowing down its natural drainage into the Klamath, is sent via a tortuous canal around the mountain back to the west, and into a holding reservoir near the crest that is visible from OR 66, called Keene Creek Reservoir. From there, the water is sent via a tunnel through the mountain, directly under Green Springs Summit, and into Emigrant Lake near Ashland. From there it flows into Bear Creek, and ultimately to the Rogue River. As a consequence of all this, it is not surprising that one asks the question: Just exactly where is the Cascade crest? I guess it's a matter of taste.

Beyond Howard Prairie, the crest shifts back and forth on either side of Dead Indian Memorial Road, until finally, near Lake of the Woods, it heads north toward Mount McLoughlin. At this point it starts behaving like a major mountain divide is supposed to.

When Howard Prairie Lake is full, the upper end is visible from Howard Prairie itself, and it acts as a magnet for water birds. American white pelicans, who share with the Cali-

fornia condor the distinction of having the greatest wingspan of any birds in North America, often gather here in the summer. So do many kinds of ducks, as well as the Canada geese that seem to be everywhere these days. Some subspecies of Canada geese still migrate to the northland for breeding purposes, but more and more of them have abandoned migration, and remain throughout the year.

The wet edges of Howard Prairie have traditionally been attractive to sandhill cranes during breeding season, and a pair can occasionally be seen striding over the grass, foraging. They also have been seen at Deadwood Prairie, about 4 miles beyond Howard Prairie.

Not far beyond the diversion dam -- the one that changed the location of the "crest" -- is Hyatt Prairie Road, on the right. Howard Prairie Recreation Area, with a marina, store, and campground, lies 3.3 miles down this road, and Hyatt Lake (see chapter on Cascade-Siskiyou

AT LEFT:
Tower delphinium

National Monument) is 3.3 miles further. Along the road between the two lakes are numerous small aspen-lined meadows. The aspens are a lovely green in the spring, and an even more lovely yellow in the fall. Along the roads in late summer, bushes of showy milkweed can be seen, a plant favored by monarch butterflies.

A bird that can usually be found at Howard Prairie Lake or at nearby Hyatt Lake, is the bald eagle. One might be perched in a dead tree along the shore, or might be in the forest on the opposite side of the lake. Scan the trees on the other side of one of the lakes for a white spot that seems to be out of place. When binoculars are focused on such a white spot, the spot often turns out to be the head of a bald eagle.

Bald eagle

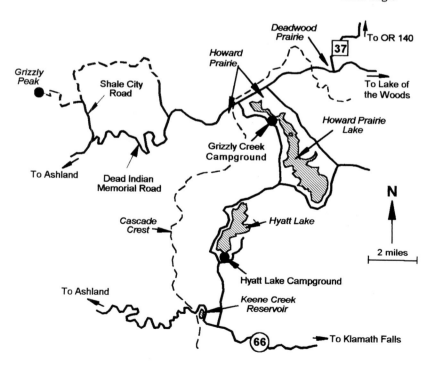

Hyatt Lake, at the "watchable wildlife" site

17 Cascade-Siskiyou National Monument

Pilot Rock, Soda Mountain, and Hyatt Lake

The Presidential Proclamation that created Cascade-Siskiyou National Monument said, in part:

> With towering fir forests, sunlit oak groves, wildflower-strewn meadows, and steep canyons, the Cascade-Siskiyou National Monument is an ecological wonder, with biological diversity unmatched in the Cascade Range. This rich enclave of natural resources is a biological crossroads -- the interface of the Cascade, Klamath, and Siskiyou ecoregions, in an area of unique geology, biology, climate, and topography.

A map of the monument in places has a checkerboard appearance, because it consists of 53,000 acres of federal land, managed by the Bureau of Land Management, distributed

---

OPPOSITE PAGE: Pilot Rock, from Pacific Crest Trail

throughout a total area of 85,000 acres. Thus, the monument is interspersed with private lands. (See map on page 119.) Users of the monument should take care not to infringe on private property rights.

I think the part of the monument lying north of the ridge that includes Soda Mountain has the greatest appeal for the general public, especially Pilot Rock, Soda Mountain Road, the Pacific Crest Trail, and Hyatt Lake. In the past, the portion of the monument south of Soda Mountain has had minimal public use, and I suspect that will not change much, partly

Red columbine

Starry false Solomon's seal

Henderson stars

Yellow salsify

because it is more difficult to reach. Two "research natural areas" that are of biological interest are located in that part of the monument.

Pilot Rock is probably the element that is most readily identified with the monument. It is highly visible as one approaches the Siskiyous either from the north or south, and of course that is how the rock got its name. The Pacific Crest Trail runs close to the base of the rock, and some energetic souls climb it, although it is no pushover. There have even been two deaths, as a result of falls.

To get to Pilot Rock, leave I-5 at Exit 6, for Mount Ashland. Take Old Highway 99 to the south, bypass the Mount Ashland Road at 0.9 mile, go under the freeway, continue 1.2 miles beyond Mount Ashland Road, and turn left on Pilot Rock Road (good gravel). At 2.0 miles on Pilot Rock Road there is a fork in the road; go right. A small parking lot lies 0.8 mile further, on the crest.

As you approach Pilot Rock on the road, you get great close-up views of it, and in June there are multitudes

Checker lily

of wildflowers along the roadside, including red columbine, common yarrow, yellow salsify, Henderson stars, and lupine. The forest increases in attractiveness as you get closer to the rock.

The **Pacific Crest Trail** (PCT) goes along the crest, and offers a delightful hike in either direction. If you go in the direction of Pilot Rock, the PCT soon veers off to the left, and contours along the mountainside. The broad trail (formerly a jeep trail) that leads to Pilot Rock goes up steeply straight ahead.

Forests, meadows, and wildflowers abound along the trail in both directions. The forest greenery has trilliums, royal Jacob's ladder, false Solomon's seal, starry false Solomon's seal, Oregon grape, and dwarf larkspur, among others.

Another access to the Pacific Crest Trail is provided by **Soda Mountain Road.** To get there, leave I-5 at Exit 14, and take OR 66 to the east for 14.6 miles. Soda Mountain road, a good gravel road, is on the right. Much of the land along the road is privately owned, so property rights should be respected. Drive slowly.

In June, the roadsides can have a remarkable variety of wildflowers, including red columbine, common camas, paintbrush, blue dicks, yellow salsify, wild rose, pussy ears, lupine,

Pale tiger swallowtail

royal Jacob's ladder, dwarf larkspur, and an odd brownish lily called checker lily. At 3.7 miles, a power line goes over the road, and the Pacific Crest Trail crosses at this point. There is enough parking along the sides of the road for a few cars, and many people park here to take day hikes on the PCT, in both directions.

A half mile or so beyond the PCT, a poor road ascends Soda Mountain to the right, which gives access to the fire lookout and communications facilities on top. The road is not one that could be recommended for ordinary cars, and it may not be kept open for that purpose as a regular thing.

An unusually high number of butterfly species have been observed in the monument -- 111 species. (The entire state of Oregon has 162 known species.) One of these, the mardon skipper, is considered rare. I have not had the luck to see a mardon skipper, but was able to get photographs of two photogenic species of butterfly -- pale tiger swallowtail, and west coast lady -- which are included in this book.

The southeast portion of **Hyatt Lake** and a little piece of the western shore are included in the national monument, and these areas receive by far the most public use of the monument lands. To my taste,

West coast lady

Hyatt Lake is more appealing than Howard Prairie Lake (see Chapter 16, "Mountain Prairies"), partly because the shore is more accessible. The road runs close to the entire west shore of the lake. Most of this land is privately owned, but in the places where BLM owns the shoreline the agency has provided gravel roads down to the edge, for day use.

In one location, a nicely-developed wildlife watching site, with picnic tables and a restroom, has been constructed by BLM. An osprey nest is visible from this part of the lake shore. In the spring, there usually have been young ospreys in the nest. Listen for the loud *cheep! cheep! cheep!* noise made by the ospreys, a sound which seems out of character for such a large raptor. Also, bald eagles are generally around, at both lakes.

Both Howard Prairie and Hyatt Lakes are reservoirs that once were mountain meadows. Since the purpose of the reservoirs is to provide water for the Bear Creek Valley, they are generally drawn down low in late summer. Having once been meadows, the shorelines are gradually sloping, and, in the case of Hyatt Lake at least, this creates a broad grassy shore that is made to order for Canada geese. Also, mountain bluebirds usually are active along these meadowy shores in summer. Migrating shorebirds find the muddy edges attractive in the fall. I even saw a sanderling here once in late September -- a bird that normally is found only at the seashore.

In late summer, the grassy shores have flowers such as chicory, bull thistle, and common mullein, all of them imports from the Old World. Tansyleaf suncups spot the meadows, making brilliant yellow patches. In the lake itself, at this time of year, floating strands of smartweed become visible, with numerous pink flower heads that stand straight up, each of them

Dwarf waterleaf

Dwarf hesperochiron

Western trillium

about the size of a person's thumb. From a distance, it may seem as if the shoreline has turned pink.

A feature of Hyatt Lake that some people find objectionable is the dead trees that were left behind when the reservoir was constructed. They stick up in the water like so many telephone poles. The cormorants, however, apparently think these "poles" were put there expressly for them, and at times it seems as if most of the poles have cormorants perched on them.

People sometimes are surprised to find cormorants at an inland location like this, because cormorants are supposed to be at the seashore. But this particular species -- the double-crested cormorant -- loves fresh water even more than salt water, and is found coast to coast at inland locations.

Besides being notable for its forests, wildflowers, birds, and butterflies, the monument has most of the mammals that are characteristic of the American west, including mountain lions, bears, deer, elk, foxes, coyotes, and bobcats. Since most of these are nocturnal, they are seldom seen, but they are around.

Tansyleaf suncup

118

There are two excellent BLM campgrounds at the southern end of the lake, both of them part of the monument, plus a couple of private campgrounds nearby. In spring, there are many wildflowers in the campgrounds and along the roads, such as western trillium, buttercups, and corn lilies, plus some "dwarfs": dwarf larkspur, dwarf waterleaf, and dwarf hesperochiron.

Coyote

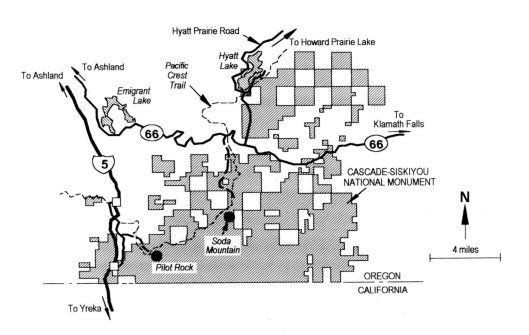

119

18 Lake of the Woods Country

A recreational paradise

There is something magical about the name, "Lake of the Woods." The name is so magical, in fact, that it has been used for 22 lakes in the United States, according to the United States Board on Geographic Names. The one in southern Oregon has got to be one of the better ones. For example, I'm not aware of any other Lake of the Woods that has a mountain as gorgeous as Mount McLoughlin standing over it.

In keeping with its beauty, the lake is extremely popular, with picnic areas, two public campgrounds, three organizational camps, a lodge, and about 200 private residences around its edges. The access road to the lake is about 36 miles east of Medford, via OR 140.

Oddly, the lake does not have any significant streams coming in or going out. Most of the inflow and outflow appears to be by groundwater seepage. In spite of this, the lake is remarkably clear. In years of high precipitation the outlet creek, Seldom Creek, may have some flow in it.

The flow of Seldom Creek, when it occurs, is toward the east through **Great Meadow.** Great Meadow is itself a scenic phenomenon, another of those great open "prairies" that grace the southern Cascades. It is highly visible from the highway as one drives along OR 140 about a mile east of the turnoff to Lake of the Woods, and is popular in winter with snowmobilers. In spring, the meadow supports a marvelous mixture of wildflowers, including common camas, lupine, and meadow penstemon.

A prominent grouping of timbered mountains to the southeast of Great Meadow, rising to over 8000 feet, marks the location of the Mountain Lakes Wilderness.

OPPOSITE PAGE:
**Mount McLoughlin and
Lake of the Woods**

AT RIGHT:
Aspens at Great Meadow in winter

Meadow penstemon

Marsh marigold

Geologically, the peaks in the wilderness are all part of one great volcano that used to contain a caldera similar to the one that holds Crater Lake. However, the Mountain Lakes volcano is much older than Crater Lake. As a result, the walls that might otherwise enclose a lake have been heavily eroded, and there are streams on all sides that drain what would otherwise be an enclosed caldera. (It is claimed that the same fate ultimately awaits Crater Lake.)

Not far from Lake of the Woods is **Fourmile Lake.** At 5744 feet, it is one of the higher lakes in Oregon. The access road is 0.6 mile west of the main access road to Lake of the Woods, on OR 140. It is 5.5 miles to the lake, on good gravel road. Along the road, there are occasionally sensational views of Mount McLoughlin to the west.

Because of its elevation, the road to the lake doesn't open until early summer, when the snow melts. There is an extensive campground along the shore that is very popular with fishermen, and also very popular with mosquitoes.

Because of its elevation, its relative isolation, and its location next to the Sky Lakes Wilderness, Fourmile Lake has more of a "wild" feel to it than does Lake of the Woods. A trail departs from the campground, that shortly enters the wilderness and connects to the Pacific Crest Trail. Wildflowers such as marsh marigolds, yellow violets, and white trilliums are scattered amongst the lodgepole pines.

The trailhead for **Mount McLoughlin** is nearby, and reachable from the Fourmile Lake Road. Mount McLoughlin, at 9495 feet, is the highest point in southern Oregon, and many people yearn to climb it. It is, however, classified as "extremely strenuous." The total elevation gain is almost 4000 feet, and involves a considerable amount of rock-scrambling toward the top. It is not for those in poor condition.

In spite of its "wild" feel, Fourmile Lake betrays the fact that it actually functions as a reservoir, because it has a highly visible drawn-down mark around its shores. In the 1920s, a rock fill dam was constructed across its outlet, and the lake was thereby considerably enlarged from its natural state. Fourmile Lake would normally send its waters down to the Klamath River, but a canal, called the "Cascade Canal," was constructed to send water back over the Cascade divide onto the western side. The water enters Fish Lake, and from there is delivered to the Medford Irrigation District.

You can see the canal, when going from OR 140 to the lake on Fourmile Lake Road. You can also see it by walking a short distance from the Summit Trailhead for the Pacific Crest Trail. This trailhead is about 3 miles west, on OR 140, from where the Fourmile Lake Road joins OR 140. Wildflowers such as Columbia windflower, and others, occur in the forest.

Columbia windflower

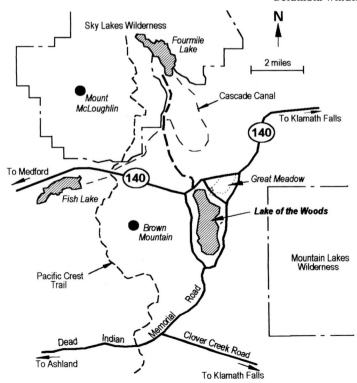

123

Osprey at nest

19 Odell Lake
And Salt Creek Falls

    Odell Lake is not the biggest lake in Oregon, nor is it the highest. But, to my eye, it is one of the most attractive. It seems to me to have a special wild quality to it, nestled as it is just to the east of the Cascade Crest.

    Yet, wild it is not. A major highway (OR 58) runs along one side, and the main line of the railroad runs along the other. Neither of these seem to detract from the lake's charm, as far as I am concerned. The railroad is invisible (although you can certainly hear it when a train goes by), and so is the highway, unless you are directly on top of it.

    Diamond Peak (8744 feet), snow-covered until mid-summer, dominates the skyline to the south, and the Diamond Peak Wilderness comes down almost to the shoreline of the lake. My guess is that the wilderness area probably would come all the way to the lake, were it not for the railroad tracks.

OPPOSITE PAGE: Salt Creek Falls

Odell Lake

A special feature possessed by this lake, in contrast to many other lakes in Oregon, is that there is no dam at the outlet, not even a small one. As a result, the lake doesn't show those unsightly "draw-down" marks around the shore that dammed lakes invariably have. The outlet stream would have to dry up altogether to produce such an effect. In the years I have known the lake I have yet to see that happen, although I suppose it is not impossible.

There are several Forest Service campgrounds around the shore, all of them attractive. The campground at the foot of the lake, where the outlet stream emerges, is especially nice, and has many shoreline sites. There is one problem, however. If there is a west wind in the afternoon, it rushes directly down the length of the lake to blow full force on the campground.

I can recall one occasion, when we were camped by the outlet stream, and the wind blew with such force that it caused patches of foam from the waves to become airborne and blow down the outlet stream as if they were alive. It was dramatic, even thrilling, and like nothing I've seen before or since, but we had to stay inside our camper to view it. On the other hand, we have been there at times when it was calm and idyllic, with innocent little candy flowers growing by the outlet stream behaving as if they had never heard of wind.

Gray jays may show up in the campgrounds, and demonstrate why they were once called "camp robbers." Also, ospreys patrol the lake on a regular basis, and it is a thrill to see one plunge into the water, to emerge with a fish. When the dive succeeds, the osprey immediately turns the fish in its talons so that the head faces forward, and then carries it off. The bird gives the distinct impression it understands the principles of aerodynamics and knows that air resistance is lessened by carrying the fish that way.

Ospreys build huge bulky nests, usually in the tops of dead trees, or on a power pole if that is all that is available. Because of such locations, osprey nests are usually highly visible.

The major tributary feeding into the lake is **Trapper Creek,** at the southwest end. This is the location of one of the campgrounds, but the creek is especially noted for being an important spawning ground for kokanee and bull trout. Bull trout have become a species of concern, partly because of competition from other fish species such as kokanee and brook trout, and party because of habitat degradation.

When the kokanee come into the shallows of the creek to spawn in late October, they steal the show with their brilliant red colors. When they appear, they can do so in large numbers. The ones in Odell Lake are not native, but were introduced years ago for fishing purposes. Bald eagles don't seem to care whether the fish are native or not, but gather in the fall to feast on the kokanee, which die after spawning.

Not too many years ago, the bull trout was considered to be a subspecies of the Dolly Varden trout, but in 1978 it was declared to be a distinct species. Purists insist that a bull

Gray jay

Rock penstemon

Huckleberry bush in autumn

Candy flower

trout is really not a trout at all, but something called a "char." It is true that they are in a different scientific genus *(Salvelinus)* from true trout *(Oncorhyncus),* but most of us are not likely to be able to tell the difference.

Bull trout are more demanding than some other kinds of trout, in their need for clean, cold, gravel spawning beds. Some restoration activity is being undertaken at Trapper Creek, to try to produce appropriate conditions for them.

A special appeal for campers at Trapper Creek Campground is the dense growth of huckleberry bushes, which forms much of the understory of the forest in the campground. Wherever the huckleberries aren't, there is low green growth that abounds with vanilla leaf, starry false Solomon's seal, Nevada pea, and bunchberry dogwood. In the greenery, occasional tiny lilies known as queen's cup occur.

Just over the crest, about 5.0 miles west of Willamette Pass, is **Salt Creek Falls.** Strictly speaking, this is slightly outside the area covered by this book (it is in Lane County), but it is such a superb spot that it calls out for inclusion. On the way to Salt Creek Falls, check the rocky cliffs next to the road for paintbrush, stonecrop, bleeding heart, and rock penstemon.

At Salt Creek Falls, the U.S. Forest Service has done an outstanding job of providing a day-use area. (A Northwest Parking Pass is required, and can be purchased on site.) Short paved trails, wheelchair-accessible, lead through the woods to the edge of a cliff where smashing views of the falls may be had. In spring, the woods are full of rhododendrons in bloom. There are even small beargrass plants tucked in among the rhododendrons, and odd-looking orchids called Mertens coralroot are scattered in the shady forest.

Nevada pea

Paved trails lead through the forest along the creek and to picnic sites. Even if the falls weren't nearby, this would be an outstanding scenic spot, and the Forest Service deserves several gold stars for its efforts.

Salt Creek Falls is a major waterfall, almost 300 feet high, and rivals Multnomah Falls in beauty and power. It seems astonishing that a creek coming from a small watershed could produce such a large waterfall. But that seems to be the way of volcanic country, where the mountains essentially act like a giant sponge, and hold incredible amounts of water. It seems that even droughts have little impact on the creeks and rivers of this kind of country, although I feel sure a series of drought years would slow them down.

A special attraction for birders is that black swifts nest on the cliffs next to the falls. For years, on repeated occasions, I have stood for hours by the falls hoping to see a black swift either coming or going, but failed. On the fifth try, I finally succeeded. Even so, I missed them as they flew out from their nests, but spotted them foraging high in the sky.

Since I've already strayed outside the strict boundary of the area covered by this book, I may as wll stray again, and mention the largest ponderosa pine tree in Oregon. This is located at LaPine State Park, about 25 miles north of Crescent on US 97, and in Deschutes County.

After turning off US 97 to the west, toward the state park, it is 4.2 miles to the turnoff to the **"Big Pine,"** on the right, onto a gravel road. It is 0.7 mile on this road to the parking lot, and then 0.2 mile on a paved trail to the tree.

It is called a "Heritage Tree," and truly was the largest ponderosa in Oregon until it lost its top in a storm. The usual criterion for "largest," means largest in total volume, but this tree is still the largest ponderosa in Oregon in diameter, at 8.6 feet, and is believed to be 500 years old.   The tree *looks* old, as if it isn't long

Mertens Coralroot

for this world, but still retains its majesty, and is in a highly scenic spot on a flat next to the cold, rushing, Deschutes River.

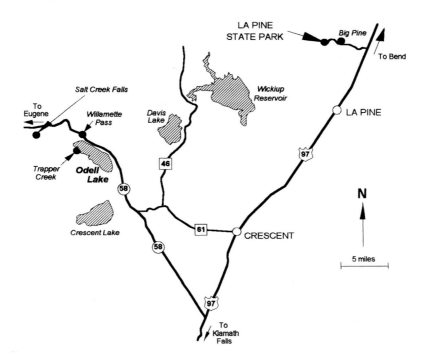

Crater Lake

20 Crater Lake

Southern Oregon's Crown Jewel

Crater Lake is a place of great beauty, and people come thousands of miles to see it. Mostly, they come to the rim, gaze at the magnificent lake in wonder, and perhaps stop at a few other rim points to admire it. They might even hike down the trail to Cleetwood Cove and take a boat trip.

Rim Village is the main point of activity, and attracts the crowds. The views of the lake are classic. A paved path leads along the edge of the rim, and here the people mingle with chipmunks, golden-mantled ground squirrels, and the ever-present Clark's nutcrackers.

Many people confuse chipmunks and golden-mantled ground squirrels, and call them both "chipmunks" because of their black and white stripes. But chipmunks are smaller than the ground squirrels and have stripes on their faces. The golden-mantled ground squirrels

---

OPPOSITE PAGE: Whitebark pine at Cloudcap

Chipmunk

Golden-mantled ground-squirrel

Clark's nutcracker

do not have stripes on their faces, although they do have stripes on their backs. Their faces, as well as their entire heads, are a golden-brown color, as their name indicates.

Nutcrackers are gray, black, and white birds that love high elevations. At the rim they fly from tree to tree, sounding their raucous calls, and seeking handouts and leftovers from the tourists. I once heard it claimed that, after the summer tourist season is over, the nutcrackers leave the lake and head for Mount Ashland. That is where crowds of people are beginning to gather for the winter ski season, with the prospect for more handouts.

Perhaps this view is fanciful, but a friend of mine said he was once standing on Pilot Rock in the fall, and observed nutcrackers flying past which appeared to be coming from the direction of Crater Lake and were heading in the direction of Mount Ashland. His observation of the birds' movements was clearly a fact, but what was in their minds is anybody's guess.

The view of the magnificent lake from the rim is certainly the major reason for making the trip to Crater Lake, but the mountain has additional rewards that come with a closer acquaintance. For one thing, it is indeed a *mountain*, a big one that rises almost into alpine territory, although it happens to be missing its top. The high point of the rim road, at Cloudcap, is the highest point you can reach anywhere in Southern Oregon by paved road, and the mountain has meadows and wildflowers and subalpine scenery that match the best anywhere.

One hardly needs to be instructed concerning how to get to Rim Village, where the lodge, gift shop, and major rim overlooks are located. Whether you come in the north or the south entrance, all roads lead to Rim Village.

Lewis monkeyflowers at Castle Crest Wildflower Garden

But, when I enter from the south, and come to the headquarters complex about 4 miles from the entrance station, what I like to do is turn on Rim Drive (East), and head for Cloudcap.

The first stop is **Castle Crest Wildflower Garden.** When I compare the throngs of people at Rim Village with the relatively few at the wildflower garden, I necessarily come to the conclusion that only a small fraction of the visitors get to the garden.

It is worth a special trip. The trail is only about a quarter-mile long. The Park Service refers to it as a "stroll," but it is a bit more than that, and a person has to be prepared for a bit of up-and-down, and some boulder-hopping. Much of the "garden" is situated on a steep slope below Castle Crest (hence, the name), and it is blessed with a number of springs.

I used to think that the springs must be coming from the water-level of the lake inside the mountain, but a little inspection of the topographic map showed me that that is impossible. The surface of the lake is at 6173 feet (average), and the springs are at the 6500-foot level. Thus, the springs are simply coming from the mountain itself, which is acting like a giant sponge.

The roster of wildflower species in late July is impressive. Heading the list are Lewis monkeyflowers, which are so vibrantly huge and colorful they look like they must have been grown in a hothouse, rather than on a rocky mountainside. At least one authority apparently

Elephant heads

Wandering daisy

thought the common name wasn't grand enough, because he gave it the name of great purple monkey-flower.

Monkeyflowers are called by that name because of the imagined ape-like faces of the flowers. In addition to the "great purple," there are also yellow monkeyflowers, along with wandering daisies, white bog-orchids, elephant heads, forget-me-nots, bleeding hearts, and blue lupine. On the dry hillside opposite to the wet springs are scarlet gilia, more lupine, spreading phlox, and sulphur flower. Altogether, it is indeed a garden.

Continuing on Rim Road (East), you come to **Vidae Falls** at 3.0 miles, a delightful lacy cascade pouring out of the mountainside. Vidae Falls, at an elevation of about 6600 feet, is also at too high an elevation for the lake inside the mountain to be its driving source. Again, it is the mountain itself which is providing all that water.

After about ten miles from the headquarters complex, you begin to enter subalpine meadowy country, with beautifully placed clumps of trees and vast views, extending all the way to the Klamath Marsh and to the Klamath Basin. At 12.3 miles, you come to the **Cloudcap** turnoff, and are soon at the parking area -- the highest place on the rim road.

The twisted whitebark pines here show how strong the winds are -- only in winter, we trust. Clark's Nutcrackers live among the pines, and apparently have a special relationship with them. The birds store pine nuts by the thousands, far more than they can eat, though they have a remarkable memory for where they stored them -- most of them, anyway. One researcher says they remember locations by utilizing nearby landmarks, and essentially use a process of triangulation to pinpoint the exact spot.

The birds cram the whitebark pine nuts into the earth or into crevices. Some of the nuts are never recovered, and eventually sprout. It is claimed that the whitebark pine is almost entirely dependent upon the nutcracker for seed dispersal, since the seeds of the whitebark lack wings.

The seeds of many other pines have wings attached, and can be dispersed by wind, but not those of the whitebark. Since whitebark pines are an important part of some of the loveliest scenery in the west, it has been said that the Clark's Nutcracker "is the caretaker of some of our most scenic vistas."

Bleeding hearts

Thus, nutcrackers seem to have solved the problem of food for the winter, because of their storage of pine nuts. So the question arises as to why so many were seen in fall flying away from Crater Lake in the fall, and headed in the direction of Mount Ashland.

A special quality of high elevation places is that they foster the evolution of tiny wildflower plants. At Cloudcap, and other high elevation locations around the lake, check the apparently barren ground between the pines. There you may find tiny volcanic daisies, lupines, and yellow daisies, all so small you may have to get down on your stomach

Volcanic daisies at Cloudcap

Vidae Falls

to examine them closely. This causes some people to give the name of "belly-flowers" to such tiny plants.

The national park has many lovely spots, but one of the loveliest is **Godfrey Glen Nature Trail,** which is located about 1.4 miles from the entrance station, as you enter from the south. The trail is barrier-free, gently graded, and passes through a wonderful hemlock-fir forest. Wildflowers such as western prince's pine, bog wintergreen, lupine, and monkshood lurk on the forest floor.

The stellar attraction is the view of Godfrey Glen, a meadow tucked into the bottom of the canyon below, surrounded by vertical cliffs and pinnacles. Barriers are provided at the best view sites. Since the cliffs are capped with loose ash, anyone approaching the edge could slip over those vertical walls with ease, a warning for those with children. Stay on the trail.

OPPOSITE PAGE:
Crater Lake in winter

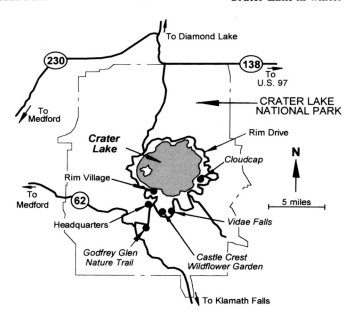

Klamath Marsh

21 Wood River Valley
And beyond, to Klamath Marsh

More than a century ago a young lieutenant named Charles Bendire, who was stationed in the Wood River Valley at Fort Klamath, wrote:

> Fort Klamath, although but 4,200 feet above sea level, has a very cool summer climate, frosts occurring in almost every month in the year. The surrounding country is very beautiful at that time. Heavy, open forests of stately pines and firs, among these the graceful and beautiful sugar pine, are found on the mountain sides and reaching well down into the green, park-like valleys. Interspersed here and there are aspen groves of various extent, their silvery trunks and light-green foliage blending artistically with the somber green of the pines.

OPPOSITE PAGE: Headwaters of Wood River, at Kimball State Park

A chamber of commerce spokesperson couldn't have said it better. But I think Lieutenant Bendire was right on target, and merely telling it like it is.

The Wood River Valley is actually a part of the Klamath Basin, as are Upper and Lower Klamath Lakes. Wood River winds its way across the flat floor of the valley from its beginning at Kimball State Park to its terminus at Agency Lake, a total distance of only 12 miles or so.

In my view, the great valley through which the river runs is one of the glories of Oregon. Thousands of tourists on their way to Crater Lake from Klamath Falls pass through the valley, and marvel at its beauty. The Wood River begins at **Kimball State Park,** a few miles north of Fort Klamath. The river appears suddenly from the base of a dry rocky slope, forms a small lake, and then runs on its way, a full-fledged river. To get to Kimball Park, go about 12 miles north on OR 62 from its junction with US 97, turn right on Sun Mountain Road, and go 2.8 miles. The park has a small campground and a picnic area. Shortly after you enter the park, there is a small parking area on the right, and a sign that says, "Wood River Headwaters."

Wood River Valley near old Fort Klamath

At the Wood River Day Use Area

A great place to enjoy the Wood River is at the **Wood River Day Use Area.** The entrance to this delightful spot is on Sun Mountain Road, 0.9 mile from the turnoff from OR 62, on the route to Kimball State Park as described above.

The day use area not only has picnic tables and restrooms, it has a great system of short trails and boardwalks that run through the aspen groves and along the edge of the river. There also are viewing platforms and benches at strategic points. All of it is wheelchair accessible.

In June, wildflowers decorate the aspen groves and grassy places, including yellow cinquefoil, white yarrow, paintbrush, western polemonium, starry false Solomon's seal, and beautiful blue Ithuriel's spear. Wildflowers also line the roadsides out in the valley itself. Look for lupine plants that have unusually dense blue heads, known as blue-pod lupine, as well as others.

About 20 miles northwest of the Wood River Valley is another great flat valley very much like it, called **Klamath Marsh.** Klamath Marsh is drained by the Williamson River, a major tributary to Upper Klamath Lake. Even though Klamath Marsh resembles the Wood River Valley, it has a different quality. Wood River Valley has many barns and ranch houses, but Klamath Marsh seems almost from a different world, with only a few barns or ranch houses visible along the edges. Most of the marsh is part of the Klamath Marsh National Wildlife Refuge, which partially explains the scarcity of human structures.

Common yarrow

Western polemonium

The name, "Klamath Marsh" has caused some confusion, because many folks expect that the marsh must be located further south, close to Upper or Lower Klamath Lakes. At one time, the refuge was named "Klamath Forest National Wildlife Refuge," perhaps in an attempt to differentiate it from the marshes further south. But the "Forest" was dropped from the name, although some of the direction signs along the highway still include the word "Forest."

To get to Klamath Marsh, go 46 miles north of Klamath Falls on US 97, and turn east on the Silver Lake Road (paved). The huge flat valley opens up within a mile, and at 4.7 miles you enter the refuge. In spring the marshy places and water channels along the road are full of waterfowl such as cinnamon teal and Canada geese. However, there are very few places where you can get off the road to park. The traffic is generally not very heavy, but much of it consists of fast-moving trucks.

The valley is about 60 to 70 square miles in extent, most of it in marsh. About 9 miles from US 97 you come to the forest on the opposite side, where there is a small parking area and a picnic table. At this point, as you look back from where you came, you realize you are in one of the most amazing places in Oregon.

The Cascade crest looms to the west, with peaks such as Mount Thielsen and Mount Scott. Far to the south is Mount McLoughlin. The valley seems almost primeval, except for the arrow-straight road on which you came. It is hard to realize that the busy travelers on U.S. 97, just 9 miles to the west, are mostly oblivious to the fact that this vast, empty, wild-looking place even exists.

The Williamson River, after it leaves the marsh, is a major stream, twice as big as the Wood River. Near **Collier State Park,** it is joined by Spring Creek, which is big enough almost to qualify as a river in its own right. The day use area of Collier State Park is 30 miles north of Klamath Falls, on US 97, and is a delightful spot with green lawns and picnic tables next to the confluence of Williamson River and Spring Creek. The green lawns have been taken over by Belding's ground squirrels, and are peppered with their holes.

If you go directly across US 97 from the day use area, past the

Ithuriel's spear

logging museum, you come to another day use area in about 0.4 mile, next to **Spring Creek.** Spring Creek here is broad and voluptuous, with grassy borders supporting yellow monkey-flowers, buttercups, and white bog-orchids. It is hard to realize that, upstream only 2 or 3 miles, there is no creek, because Spring Creek is another of those astonishing Oregon streams that bursts full-blown from a dry hillside. The creek has grassy borders next to its source, with wild strawberries and dandelions.

To see the source of Spring Creek for yourself, go 2.9 miles north of the Collier State Park day-use area on US 97, to Forest Road 9732, and turn' west. Road 9732 is a

Wild strawberries at source of Spring Creek

good gravel road, and brings you in about 4.0 miles to a day-use area next to Spring Creek's source. Take the short path next the rest room, to get to the source. The transition from dry pine forest to the lush greenery around the springs is sudden and startling, although it is a transition frequently encountered in central Oregon.

OPPOSITE PAGE: Path through aspen grove at Wood River Day Use Area

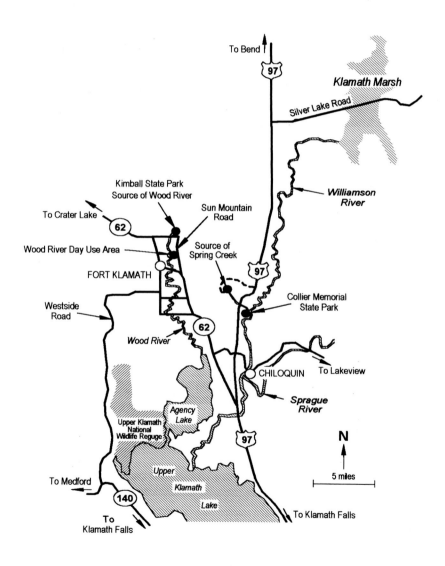

American white pelicans at Howard Bay

22 Upper Klamath Lake

Another Oregon gem

Upper Klamath Lake is the largest freshwater lake in Oregon, and surely one of the most beautiful anywhere. The major tributary is the Williamson River, which supplies almost half of the lake's input. The second largest is the Wood River. (See Chapter 21, **Wood River Valley.**)

Although the lake is beautiful from every vantage point, it probably is most attractive on the western side. At **Howard Bay,** OR 140 runs directly along the edge of the lake (almost *in* the lake, some would say). There are a couple of parking places that give an opportunity to stop and look at the lake and the birds that are almost sure to be there. American white pelicans are often present in summer, and in the spring the numbers of western and Clark's grebes can be astonishing. It has been claimed that the breeding colonies of these two

---

OPPOSITE PAGE: Upper Klamath Lake at Rocky Point

Washington lily

closely-related species at Upper Klamath Lake are the largest in the country. Gulls and terns often fly by.

One of the best-known sites along the lake is **Rocky Point**, which lies 3 miles or so north of OR 140, on Westside Road. (The intersection of OR 140 and Westside Road is about 45 miles east of Medford, and 25 miles northwest of Klamath Falls.) Rocky Point has a collections of cabins, a resort, and a public boat-launching ramp. From the boat-launching ramp a portion of the lake is visible, including the edge of the vast marsh that adjoins the northern part of the lake.

North of Rocky Point, Westside Road passes through beautiful forest, with occasional views of the marsh. Washington lilies occur here in early July, sometimes in surprisingly dry locations.

South of Rocky Point, OR 140 passes through extensive groves of aspen, which turn a brilliant yellow in October. Some of the trees in fall take on a golden-bronze color. There are great meadows along the road, showing that at one time there were lake-bottoms here.

Eight miles south of Westside Road, on OR 140, is the road leading to **Eagle Ridge Park,** to the east. It is four miles or so on gravel road to the park. For the last mile or so the route runs close to Shoalwater Bay Marsh, which is a wildlife area managed by the State of Oregon. At some seasons there can be many ducks and grebes here, and, at times when the water is low, as in the fall, there are likely to be shorebirds. The views of Mount McLoughlin across Shoalwater Bay are some of the best in the area.

Howard Bay comes next, 5 miles south of the road to Eagle Ridge Park. Not only are there great opportunities to see birds here, this is one of the best views of the lake. The lake is 12 miles wide and 25

Aspen trees in autumn

miles long in its greatest dimensions. Its depth, however, is not great, and is less than 20 feet in most places.

The outlet of the lake is at the southern extremity, and is called **Link River,** because it links Upper Klamath Lake and Lake Ewauna. Link River is only about 1.5 miles long, and is paralleled by a gravel road which doubles as a nature trail. (There is a parking area next to the river at the north end.) Horses and bicycles are not permitted.

The scenic qualities of the Link River trail are diminished somewhat by the presence of a low dam and a power plant.

Western grebe

Nevertheless, it makes a nice walk, with water birds such as grebes, goldeneyes, and mergansers in the river, and land birds in the riparian growth along the trail.

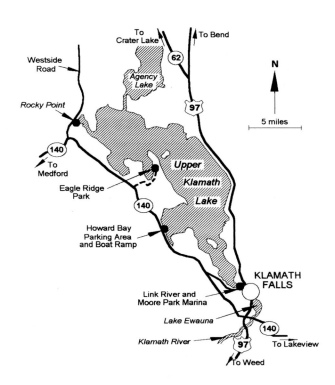

Snow geese

23 Klamath Basin

The lakes that once were

The American West specializes in magnificent vistas, and those in the Klamath Basin are among the best. Mount Shasta dominates the view to the southwest, while Mount Mcloughlin is visible to the north. Lesser peaks rim the basin elsewhere.

In former times, the lower part of the basin was filled with two great lakes, Tule Lake and Lower Klamath Lake. At that time these lakes lay partially in Oregon and partially in California. In the early part of the 20th century, the lakes were mostly drained and converted to agriculture, and today their remnants are essentially confined to the California side. The town of Tulelake would be below water if the original Tule Lake still existed.

OPPOSITE PAGE:
Mount Shasta and part of Klamath Basin, seen from Hamaker Mountain

Ruddy duck

Yellow-headed blackbird

American avocet

The two lakes don't connect as a usual thing, although in the past they did so during periods of extreme flood, and are connectible today by means of an elaborate system of canals and a tunnel. Tule Lake is fed by Lost River, which has its beginnings in the Devils Garden, an expanse of rocks and junipers lying on the high ground to the east. The waters from Devils Garden are collected into Clear Lake, a reservoir only 20 miles east of Tule Lake. From its point of origin, Lost River flows to the north and makes a great circuit through Southern Oregon, until it turns south and flows into Tule Lake.

The area is known for its huge numbers of migrating geese, swans, and ducks, and for its wintertime population of bald eagles. In a recent survey, the number of geese, swans, and ducks in migration was estimated at 1,100,000. The basin has been formally designated as a bird area of global importance.

The number of wintering eagles may range from 500 to 1000, depending upon weather and upon available prey, and is believed to be the largest wintertime concentration of bald eagles in the lower 48 states. Every year, on a weekend in February, the Klamath Basin Audubon Society sponsors the **Bald Eagle Conference.** As part of the program, participants gather at dawn to observe the eagles fly out to forage in the basin.

In the channels at the **Lower Klamath Refuge**, western grebes, ruddy ducks, and other water birds can be observed. A yellow-headed blackbird may groan out his weird "love song," which has been described as "a wail of despairing agony which would do credit to a dying catamount." (Dawson, 1923.)

One of the best places to observe water birds is along CA 161, known as "Stateline Road" because of its position on the Oregon-California border. In the shallow area toward the eastern end of the road, called **White Lake**, great numbers of ducks, geese, and swans may be seen. (White Lake is about 4.0 miles east of the auto tour entrance of Lower Klamath Refuge.) This is also a good place to see some tall spindly-legged shorebirds -- American avocets, and black-necked stilts. Snow geese often fill the sky with their huge flocks, and then settle down in the nearby flooded fields to forage.

Pronghorn

If you are really lucky, you might spot a herd of pronghorns, since they sometimes come down to the farm fields. I once spotted a herd right along Stateline Road, near the town of Tulelake.

Sheepy Ridge is a rocky ridge that divides the two lakes. The refuge **visitor center** is located next to Sheepy Ridge, about 3 miles south of CA 161, on Hill Road. A short trail ascends Sheepy Ridge behind the visitor center. The trail is only a quarter-mile or so long, and takes you up to a stone "lookout" that was constructed by the CCC (Civilian Conservation Corps) in the 1930s. It's hard to conceive what useful purpose the "lookout" may have served, but it is a delightful destination, and gives a marvelous view over the **Tule Lake** basin.

Mule deer near Sheepy Ridge

Day-use area next to John C. Boyle Reservoir

By the way, Sheepy Ridge got its name because there once were bighorn sheep here, but they were extirpated in the early 20th century. An attempt in the 1970s to get them reestablished failed. Mule deer thrive along Sheepy Ridge, however, and are often seen.

The Klamath River, after it leaves the vicinity of the city of Klamath Falls, winds back and forth over the flat floor of the Klamath Basin, heads west past the small town of Keno, and then plunges into a deep canyon, in which it remains for the rest of its journey to the ocean. Just as it enters the canyon, a large dam has been constructed, which creates the **John C. Boyle Reservoir.**

Most reservoirs have unsightly "drawdown" marks along the sides. Not this one. In fact, at the location where you encounter it, along OR 66, about 5.7 miles west of Keno, you might not even realize you are looking at a reservoir. OR 66 crosses the waters of the reservoir on a bridge at this point, and the reservoir is so narrow, it just looks like a regular part of the Klamath River. To the right, as you cross the bridge going west, is a large open expanse of water that often has many kinds of water birds, including white pelicans. To the left, just after you cross the bridge, is a delightful little day-use area, located on a tree-shaded flat next the river.

For a special view of the basin, you might take the paved road (occasional potholes) to the top of **Hamaker Mountain,** which leaves OR 66 about 1.0 mile west of Keno. It is 8.2 miles to the summit. The top of the mountain can not exactly be described as "beautiful," because it is covered with huge antennas. But the views to the south and east are sensational, and if you can avoid looking at the antennas, it is worth a side trip.

Highway 140 cuts across the southern part of Klamath County, traversing country which alternately consists of forested mountains and beautiful flat, green valleys. The town of Bonanza lies in one of these valleys, called Langell Valley, about 20 miles east of Klamath Falls. To get there, you turn off of Highway 140 at Dairy, about 14 miles east of Klamath Falls, and take Highway 70 to Bonanza.

From Bonanza, you can get a small taste of what it is like in the vast **Devils Garden,** most of which lies just over the Oregon border in Northern California. To enjoy this country, you must love junipers, sagebrush, and rocks, which are not everyone's cup of tea.

154

In Bonanza, take the road to Gerber Reservoir (paved), which lies about 19 miles to the east. Wildflowers such as sagebrush buttercups and spring gold find a place here.

Gerber Reservoir, operated by the Bureau of Land Management, has a couple of nice campgrounds, and is popular with boaters. The reservoir itself is not particularly attractive, but the area has some interesting features known as the **Gerber Potholes.** These are shallow bod-

"Pothole" near Gerber Reservoir

ies of water which dry up by midsummer, but which, in spring, provide nesting territories for ducks, geese, and sandhill cranes. Three of the more attractive potholes can be reached from

Sprague River picnic area, near "Devils Garden"

the entrance road to Gerber Reservoir, by taking the gravel road to the left. The ponds all lie within the first mile on both sides of this road.

The name "Devils Garden" is a popular one. The Board of Geographic Names lists 22 areas with this name in the U.S., eight of them in Oregon. (Two of them are shown on the map on Page 156.) There is a small "Devils Garden" right on Highway 140, about 52 miles east of Klamath Falls.

The centerpiece of this particular "garden"

Sagebrush buttercup at Gerber Potholes

is known as the **Sprague River Picnic Area,** about 4.1 miles east of Bly. On the surrounding uplands, the landscape consists of juniper, sagebrush, and rocks. The picnic area lies in the bottom of a gorge reached by a short, narrow paved road. The bottom of the gorge is relatively level, with a beautiful stream, the Sprague River, flowing through it. There are picnic sites, green lawns, and a short loop trail that bridges the river twice. The contrast between the lushness of the valley, and the austerity of the surrounding junipers and sagebrush comes as a bit of a surprise.

OPPOSITE PAGE:

Tule Lake, from the "lookout" above the visitor center

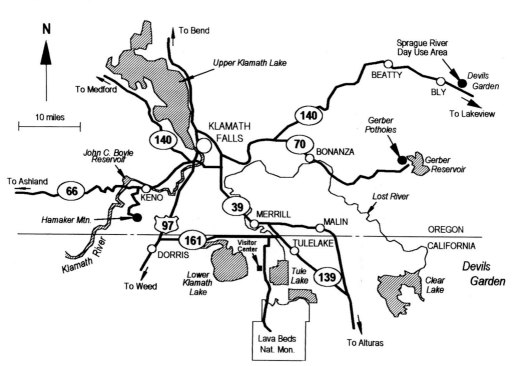

156

Appendix A - REFERENCES

Arno, Stephen F., and Hammerly, Ramona P. 1977. *Nothwest Trees.* The Mountaineers, Seattle, WA.

A Trail Guide to Castle Crest. Crater Lake Natural History Association, Crater Lake, OR.

Atwood, Kay. 1978. *Illahe: The Story of Settlement in the Rogue River Canyon.* Oregon State University Press, Corvallis, OR.

Baake, Tom. 2002. *Out Our Back Door: Driving Tours and Day-Hikes in Oregon's Coos Region.* Westways Press, Coos Bay, OR.

Bannan, Jan. 1993. *Oregon State Parks, a Complete Recreation Guide.* The Mountaineers, Seattle, WA.

Bastasch, Rick. 1998. *Waters of Oregon.* Oregon State University Press, Corvallis, Oregon.

Begnoche, Don. 1999. *Siskiyou Sundays, A Tour of Southwestern Oregon.* Don Begnoche.

Bent, Arthur Cleveland. 1939. *Life Histories of North American Woodpeckers.* Smithsonian Institution United States National Museum.

Bernstein, Art. 2001. *Hiking Oregon's Southern Cascades and Siskiyous.* Globe Pequot Press, Guilford, CT.

Booth, Percy T. 1997. *Until the Last Arrow.* B & B Publishing, Coos Bay, OR.

Cascade-Siskiyou National Monument -- Draft Resource Management Plan/Environmental Impact Statement. (2 vols.) U.S. Department of the Interior, Bureau of Land Management, Medford District Office, Medford, OR.

Contreras, Alan. 1998. *Birds of Coos County, Oregon: Status and Distribution.* Cape Arago Adubon Society, North Bend, OR.

Crater Lake National Park, Oregon. 2002. National Park Service, Washington, DC.

Csuti, Blair, et al. 2001. *Atlas of Oregon Wildlife.* Oregon State University Press, Corvallis, OR.

Dawson, William Leon. 1923. *The Birds of California.* South Moulton Co., San Diego, CA.

Douthit, Nathan. 1999. *A Guide to Oregon South Coast History.* Oregon State University Press, Corvallis, OR.

Friedman, Ralph. 1990. *In Search of Western Oregon.* Caxton Printers, Caldwell, Idaho.

Gilkey, Helen M., and Dennis, La Rea J. 2001. *Handbook of Northwestern Plants.* Oregon State University Press, Corvallis, OR.

Hickman, James C. (ed.) **1993.** *The Jepson Manual -- Higher Plants of California.* University of California Press, Berkeley, CA.

Jensen, Edward C., et al. 2000. *Manual of Oregon Trees and Shrubs.* John Bell and Associates, Corvallis, OR.

Jensen, Edward C., and Ross, Charles R. 1994. *Trees to Know in Oregon.* Oregon State University Extension Service, Corvallis, OR.

Johnson, Daniel M, et al. 1985. *Atlas of Oregon Lakes.* Oregon State University Press, Corvallis, OR.

Kemper, John. 2002. *Southern Oregon's Bird Life.* Outdoor Press, Medford, OR.

Kennedy, David, et al. 2002. *The Bear Creek Greenway Trail Guide.* Nature Works Press, Talent, OR.

LaLande, Jeff. *Butte Falls Discovery Loop Tour.* Butte Falls Economic Development Commission, Butte Falls, OR

La Monte, Francesca. 1945. *North American Game Fishes.* Doubleday and Co., Garden City, NY.

Lithia Park Woodland Trail -- Guide to Trees and Shrubs. 1996. Ashland Parks and Recreation Department, Ashland, OR.

Mathews, Daniel. 1999. *Cascade-Olympic Natural History -- A Trailside Reference* (2nd ed.). Raven Editions, Portland, OR.

McArthur, Lewis. 1992. *Oregon Geographic Names.* Oregon Historical Society Press, Portland, OR.

National Register of Big Trees. 2003. American Forests, Washington DC

Niehaus, Theodore F., and Ripper, Charles L. 1976. *A Field Guide to Pacific States Wildflowers.* Houghton Mifflin Co., Boston, MA.

O'harra, Marjorie. 1986. *Lithia Park.* Ashland Parks and Recreation Department, Ashland, OR.

Oregon Caves Official Map and Guide. 1998. National Park Service, Washington, DC.

Oregon Parks and Heritage Guide. 2002-2003. Oregon Parks and Recreation Dept. Salem, OR.

Peattie, Donald Culross. 1980. *A Natural History of Western Trees.* University of Nebraska Press, Lincoln, NE.

Plants of Oregon -- Interactive Keys and Color Photos. (CD) 2001. Flora ID West, Pendleton, OR.

Plumb, Gregory A. 1983. *Waterfalls of the Pacific Northwest.* The Writing Works, Seattle, WA.

Pojar, Jim, and MacKinnon, Andy (eds.) 1994. *Plants of the Pacific Northwest Coast.* Lone Pine Publishing, Vancouver, BC.

Reyes, Chris (ed.). 1994. *The Table Rocks of Jackson County: Islands in the Sky.* Last Minute Publications, Ashland, OR.

159

Ross, Robert A., and Chambers, Henrietta L. 1995. *Wildflowers of the Western Cascades.* Timber Press, Portland, OR.

Schaffer, Jeffrey P. 1983. *Crater Lake National Park and Vicinity.* Wilderness Press, Berkeley, CA.

Spellenberg, Richard. 1979. *The Audubon Society Field Guide to North American Wildflowers -- Western Region.* Alfred A. Knopf, New York, NY.

Stewart, Charles. 1994. *Wildflowers of the Olympics and Cascades.* Nature Education Enterprises, Port Angeles, WA>

Strickler, Dee. 1993. *Wayside wildflowers of the Pacific Northwest.* The Flower Press, Columbia Falls, MT.

Sudworth, George B. 1908. *Forest Trees of the Pacific Slope.* U.S. Dept. of Agriculture, Forest Service, Washington, DC.

The Siskiyou Loop (brochure). USDA National Forest Service, Rogue River National Forest, Medford, OR.

Taylor, G.H., and Hatton, R.R. 1999. *The Oregon Weather Book: A State of Extremes.* Oregon State University Press, Corvallis, OR

Taylor, Ronald J. 1990. *Northwest Weeds -- The Ugly and Beautiful Villains of Fields, Gardens, and Roadsides.* Mountain Press Publishing Co., Missoula, MT.

Taylor, R.J., and Douglas, G. W. 1995. *Mountain Plants of the Pacific Northwest.* Mountain Press Publishing Co., Missoula, MT.

Tice, Kevin K. 1995. *The Rogue River Guide.* Mountain N'Air Books, La Crescenta, CA.

Webber, Bert and Margie. 1998. *Awesome Caverns of Marble in the Oregon Caves National Monument -- Documentary.* Webb Research Group Publishers, Medford, OR.

Wiedemann, A.M., Dennis, L.R.J., and Smith, F.H. 1999. *Plants of the Oregon Coastal Dunes.* Oregon State University Press, Corvallis, OR.

Wiesen, Pamela (ed.). 2001. *The Complete Guide to America's National Parks -- Eleventh Edition.* Fodor's Travel Publications, New York, NY.

The World Almanac, 2002. World Almanac Books, New York, NY.

Wuerthner, George. 2001. *Oregon's Best Wildflower Hikes -- Northwest Region.* Westcliffe Publishers, Englewood, CO.

Zika, Peter F. 2003. *A Crater Lake National Park Vascular Checklist.* Crater Lake Natural History Association, Crater Lake, OR.

Appendix B - SCIENTIFIC NAMES OF WILDFLOWERS

Below, arranged by the numbers of the pages on which they appear, are the common names, scientific names, and family names of the wildflowers that are illustrated in this book. (Cultivated flowers at places like Azalea Park in Brookings and Lithia Park in Ashland are not included in the list.) Family names are shown in parentheses. Common names, of course, are highly variable, and in some cases I have shown several of the common names that seem to be in use. The word "alien" is added, if the species is not native.

Scientific names are intended to be invariable everywhere in the world, but even here there can be some confusion, partly because taxonomic research causes certain reclassifications (and renaming) to be desirable, and partly because authorities may disagree. Below, I have shown former and/or alternate scientific names in square brackets.

In some cases identification beyond the genus, as in the case of the checkermallows (*Sidalcea*), seems not be useful for the purposes of this book. In such a case, the scientific name is given as in the following example: *Sidalcea* sp. Here, "sp." is an abbreviation for "species" (singular: "sp.", plural: "spp."). The *Audubon Society Field Guide* states, for example, "The many checkermallows with pink flowers . . . are difficult to distinguish and differentiated only by technical characteristics."

Page No.	Common name(s)	Scientific name, and family
4	Salal	*Galtheria shallon* (Heath family: *Ericaceae*)
4	Western azalea	*Rhododendron occidentale* (Heath family: *Ericaceae*)
7	Foxglove (alien)	*Digitalis purpurea* (Figwort family: *Scrophulariaceae*)
9	Ox-eye daisy (alien)	*Leucanthemum vulgare* [*Chrysanthemum leucanthemum*] (Sunflower family: *Asteraceae* [*Compositae*])
10	Perennial sweetpea (alien)	*Lathyrus latifolius* (Pea family: *Fabaceae* [*Leguminosae*])
10	Seaside daisy Seaside fleabane	*Erigeron glaucous* (Sunflower family: *Asteraceae* [*Compositae*])
10	Hedge morning glory Hedge bindweed	*Calystegia sepium* (Morning glory family: *Convolvulaceae*)
11	Beach strawberry Coastal strawberry	*Fragaria chiloensis* (Rose family: *Rosaceae*)
11, 15	Douglas iris	*Iris douglasiana* (Iris family: *Iridaceae*)
27	Redwood sorrel Oregon oxalis	*Oxalis oregana* (Oxalis family: *Oxalidaceae*)
30	Tiger lily Columbia lily Oregon lily	*Lilium columbianum* (Lily family: *Liliaceae*)
30	Checkermallow	*Sidalcea* sp. (Mallow family: *Malvaceae*)
32	Pacific Rhododendron California rose-bay	*Rhododendron macrophyllum* (Heath family: *Ericaceae*)

Page No.	Common name(s)	Scientific name, and family
32	Bunchberry dogwood Dwarf dogwood	*Cornus canadensis* (Dogwood family: *Cornaceae*)
34	Cream fawn lily Lemon fawn lily Cream-colored adder's tongue	*Erythronium citrinum* (Lily family: *Liliaceae*)
36	Long-beaked Storksbill (alien) Filaree (alien)	*Erodium botrys* (Geranium family: *Geraniaceae*)
36	Seep-spring monkeyflower Common monkeyflower	*Mimulus guttatus* (Figwort family: *Scrophulariaceae*)
36	Spring gold Gold star	*Crocidium multicaule* (Sunflower family: *Asteraceae* [*Compositae*])
36	Larkspur Delphinium	*Delphinium* sp. (Buttercup family: *Ranunculaceae*)
38	Common madia Showy tarweed	*Madia elegans* (Sunflower family: *Asteraceae* [*Compositae*])
38	Golden iris Del Norte County iris	*Iris innominata* (Iris family: *Iridaceae*)
38	Douglas iris (see **Page 11**)	
38	Broadleaf stonecrop Pacific sedum	*Sedum spathulifolium* (Stonecrop family: *Crassulaceae*)
39	Yellow-leaved iris Slender-tubed iris	*Iris chrysophylla* (Iris family: *Iridaceae*)
43	Calypso orchid Fairy Slipper	*Calypso bulbosa* (Orchid family: *Orchidaceae*)
43	Woodland phlox Northern phlox	*Phlox adsurgens* (Phlox family: *Polemoniaceae*)
43	California ground-cone	*Boshniakia strobilacea* (Broomrape family: *Orobanchaceae*)
44	Siskiyou iris	*Iris bracteata* (Iris family: *Iridaceae*)
44	Sickle-leaved onion Scytheleaf onion	*Allium falcifolium* (Lily family: *Liliaceae*)
44	Long-leaved phlox	*Phlox longifolia* (Phlox family: *Polemoniaceae*)
44	Hooker Indian pink Stringflower	*Silene hookeri* (Pink family: *Caryophyllaceae*)
45	Red-flowering currant	*Ribes sanguineum* (Gooseberry family: *Grossulariaceae*)

Page No.	Common name(s)	Scientific name, and family
45	Deltoid balsamroot	*Balsamorhiza deltoidea* (Sunflower family: *Asteraceae* [*Compositae*])
46	Cobra lily California pitcher-plant	*Darlingtonia californica* (Pitcher-plant family: *Sarraceniaceae*)
47	Purple-eyed grass Grass widow Satin-flower	*Sisyrinchium douglasii* [*Olysynium douglasii*] (Iris family: *Iridaceae*)
48	Henderson fawn lily	*Erythronium hendersonii* (Lily family: *Liliaceae*)
50	Henderson shooting stars Mosquito bills Sailor caps	*Dodecatheon hendersonii* (Primrose family: *Primulaceae*)
50	Large-flowered blue-eyed Mary Large innocence Chinese pagodas	*Collinsia grandiflora* (Figwort family: *Scrophulariaceae*)
50	Pussy ears Tolmie cat-ears Tolmie startulip	*Calochortus tolmiei* (Lily family: *Liliaceae*)
50	Rosy plectritis Shortspur seablush	*Plectritis congesta* (Valerian family: *Valerianaceae*)
52	Miner's lettuce Indian lettuce	*Claytonia perfoliata* [*Montia perfoliata*] (Purslane family: *Portulaceae*)
58	Creeping buttercup (alien)	*Ranunculus repens* (Buttercup family: *Ranunculaceae*)
58	Blue dicks	*Dichelostemma capitatum* [*Dichelostemma pulchellum*] (Lily family: *Liliaceae*)
59	Oregon grape Tall Oregon-grape Hollyleaf mahonia	*Berberis aquifolium* [*Mahonia aquifolium*] (Barberry family: *Berberidaceae*)
61	Dog rose (alien)	*Rosa canina* (Rose family: *Rosaceae*)
62	California poppy	*Escholtzia californica* (Poppy family: *Papaveraceae*)
62	Purple deadnettle Red henbit	*Lamium purpureum* (Mint family: *Lamiaceae* [*Labiatae*])
65	Baby blue eyes Large-flowered nemophila	*Nemophila menziesii* (Waterleaf family: *Hydrophyllaceae*)
66	Gentner fritillaria Gentner missionbells	*Fritillaria gentneri* (Lily family: *Liliaceae*)
67	Gold fields California goldfields	*Lasthenia californica* [*Lasthenia chrysostoma*] (Sunflower family: *Asteraceae* [*Compositae*])

Page No.	Common name(s)	Scientific name, and family
95	Sulphur flower Sulphur buckwheat	*Eriogonum umbellatum* (Buckwheat family: *Polygonaceae*)
95	Coyote mint Western balm	*Monardella odoratissima* (Mint family: *Lamiaceae [Labiatae]*)
96	Ground rose	*Rosa spithamea* (Rose family: *Rosaceae*)
101	Pacific dogwood	*Cornus nuttallii* (Dogwood family: *Cornaceae*)
101	Western trumpet honeysuckle Orange honeysuckle Climbing honeysuckle	*Lonicera ciliosa* (Honeysuckle family: *Caprifoliaceae*)
102	Queen's cup Bead lily One-flowered clintonia	*Clintonia uniflora* (Lily family: *Liliaceae*)
103	Spotted coralroot	*Corallorhiza maculata* (Orchid family: *Orchidaceae*)
106	Winter vetch (alien) Hairy vetch (alien)	*Vicia villosa* (Pea family: *Fabaceae [Leguminosae]*)
107	Royal Jacob's ladder Royal polemonium Great polemonium	*Polemonium carneum* (Phlox family: *Polemoniaceae*)
107	Wild ginger Long-tailed wild ginger	*Asarum caudatum* (Pipevine family: *Aristolochiaceae*)
107	Western trillium Pacific trillium Western wake robin	*Trillium ovatum* (Lily family: *Liliaceae*)
107	Woodland star	*Lithophragma affine* (Saxifrage family: *Saxifragaceae*)
108	Striped coralroot Hooded coralroot	*Corallorhiza striata* (Orchid family: *Orchidaceae*)
109	Common camas	*Camassia quamash* (Lily family: *Lilaceae*)
110	Tower delphinium Mountain larkspur Tall larkspur	*Delphinium glaucum* (Buttercup family: *Ranunculaceae*)
114	Red columbine Western columbine	*Aquilegia formosa* (Buttercup family: *Ranunculaceae*)
114	Starry false Solomon's seal Starry false lily of the valley	*Smilacina stellata [Maianthemum stellata]* (Lily family: *Liliaceae*)

165

Page No.	Common name(s)	Scientific name, and family
114	Henderson stars Henderson triteleia	*Triteleia hendersonii* (Lily family: *Liliaceae*)
114	Yellow salsify (alien)	*Tragopogon dubius* (Sunflower family: *Asteraceae* [*Compositae*])
115	Checker lily Mission bells Chocolate lily	*Fritillaria affinis* [*Fritillaria lanceolata*] (Lily family: *Liliaceae*)
117	Dwarf waterleaf Ballhead waterleaf	*Hydrophyllum capitatum* (Waterleaf family: *Hydrophyllaceae*)
117	Dwarf hesperochiron	*Hesperochiron pumilus* (Waterleaf family: *Hydrophyllaceae*)
118	Western trillium (see page **107**)	
118	Tansyleaf suncup Tansyleaf evening primrose	*Camissonia tanacetifolia* (Evening primrose family: *Onagraceae*)
122	Meadow penstemon Rydberg penstemon	*Penstemon rydbergi* (Figwort family: *Scrophulariaceae*)
122	Marsh marigold	*Caltha leptosepala* (Buttercup family: *Ranunculaceae*)
123	Columbia windflower Wind anemone Western white anemone	*Anemone deltoidea* (Buttercup family: *Ranunculaceae*)
127	Rock penstemon Cliff penstemon Cliff beardtongue	*Penstemon rupicola* (Figwort family: *Scrophulariaceae*)
127	Candy flower Western spring beauty Siberian miner's lettuce	*Claytonia sibirica* [*Montia sibirica*] (Purslane family: *Portulacaceae*)
128	Nevada pea Sierra Nevada pea	*Lathyrus nevadensis* (Pea family: *Fabaceae* [*Leguminosae*])
129	Mertens coralroot Western coral root	*Corallorhiza mertensiana* (Orchid family: *Orchidaceae*)
133	Lewis monkeyflower Pink monkey-flower Great purple monkey-flower	*Mimulus lewisii* (Figwort family: *Scrophulariaceae*)
134	Elephant heads Pink elephants	*Pedicularis groenlandica* (Figwort family: *Scrophulariaceae*)
134	Wandering daisy (see page **88**)	
135	Bleeding hearts Pacific bleeding heart	*Dicentra formosa* (Poppy family: *Papaveracaea* [*Fumariaceae*])

Baneberry near Grizzly Peak, in August

INDEX